# THE LIMITS
# OF LIBERAL
# DEMOCRACY

Politics and Religion at the End of Modernity

# SCOTT H. MOORE

## IVP Academic

An imprint of InterVarsity Press
Downers Grove, Illinois

InterVarsity Press
P.O. Box 1400, Downers Grove, IL 60515-1426
World Wide Web: www.ivpress.com
E-mail: email@ivpress.com

InterVarsity Press® is the book-publishing division of InterVarsity Christian Fellowship/USA®, a student movement
active on campus at hundreds of universities, colleges and schools of nursing in the United States of America, and a
member movement of the International Fellowship of Evangelical Students. For information about local and regional
activities, write Public Relations Dept., InterVarsity Christian Fellowship/USA, 6400 Schroeder Rd., P.O. Box 7895,
Madison, WI 53707-7895, or visit the IVCF website at <www.intervarsity.org>.

All Scripture quotations, unless otherwise indicated, are taken from the New American Standard Bible®, copyright
1960, 1962, 1963, 1968, 1971, 1972, 1973, 1975, 1977, 1995 by The Lockman Foundation. Used by permission.

Portions of chapter eight originally appeared as "Hospitality as an Alternative to Tolerance," Communio 27,
no. 3 (2000). Used by permission.

Design: Cindy Kiple
Images: church: Clipart.com
government building: Clipart.com

ISBN 978-0-8308-2893-7

Printed in the United States of America ∞

**Library of Congress Cataloging-in-Publication Data**

Moore, Scott H., 1964-
    The limits of liberal democracy: politics and religion at the end
of modernity / Scott H. Moore.
        p. cm.
    Book is a series of conversations that began during a sabbatical
    year at the Center for Philosophy of Religion at the University of
    Notre Dame and produced an essay, "The end of convenient
    stereotypes" that was originally published in the journal Pro
    Ecclesia, winter 1998 & reprinted in, The end of democracy II: a
    crisis of legitimacy (Spence Pub., 1999) edited as "Hospitality as an
    alternative to tolerance" in Communio 27, no. 3, fall 2000. Includes
    bibliographical references and index. ISBN 978-0-8308-2893-7 (pbk.:
    alk. paper)
    1. Christianity and politics. 2. Democracy—Religious
aspects—Christianity. 3. Liberalism—Religious
aspects—Christianity. I. Title.
BR115.P7M558 2008
261.7—dc22
                                                                          2008046025

| P | 21 | 20 | 19 | 18 | 17 | 16 | 15 | 14 | 13 | 12 | 11 | 10 | 9 | 8 | 7 | 6 | 5 | 4 | 3 | 2 | 1 |
|---|----|----|----|----|----|----|----|----|----|----|----|----|---|---|---|---|---|---|---|---|---|
| Y | 27 | 26 | 25 | 24 | 23 | 22 | 21 | 20 | 19 | 18 | 17 | 16 | 15 | 14 | 13 | 12 | 11 | 10 | 09 | | | |

*for*

*Emily Anne,*

*Benjamin,*

*Hannah,*

*Samuel*

*and Andrew*

# CONTENTS

# ACKNOWLEDGMENTS

This volume is the product of a series of unexpected conversations which led to a surprising avenue of reflection and inquiry. These conversations began during a sabbatical year at the Center for Philosophy of Religion at the University of Notre Dame and produced an essay ("The End of Convenient Stereotypes") that was originally published in the journal *Pro Ecclesia* 7, no. 1 (1998) and then reprinted in the collection *The End of Democracy II: A Crisis of Legitimacy* (Spence Publishing, 1999) edited by Mitch Muncy. Portions of chapter eight originally appeared as "Hospitality as an Alternative to Tolerance" in *Communio* 27, no. 3 (2000). Along the way, both Michael Baxter and Richard John Neuhaus responded (either in person or in print) to earlier versions of some of this material, and I am grateful for their insights, attention and good will.

I am quite fortunate to work within three extraordinary academic units at Baylor University—the philosophy department, the Great Texts program and the honors college. My work would not be possible were it not for the genuinely remarkable colleagues that I have in these programs. I am particularly indebted to Michele Anderson and Paulette Edwards for their untiring patience and daily assistance with the myriad of administrative duties and tasks that come the way of a department chair.

Many friends and colleagues have helped me think about the issues addressed in this volume. To name them all would be impossible, but I am especially grateful to the following friends who have read drafts, corrected misunderstandings and sought (not always successfully) to set me straight: Bob Baird, Michael Beaty, Michael Budde, David Burrell, Darin Davis, Fred Freddoso, Stanley Hauerwas, Tom Hibbs, Victor Hinojosa, David Jeffrey, Bob Kruschwitz, Beth Newman, David Solomon, Roger Ward and Ralph Wood have each played such a role for me. Two dear friends and mentors, A. J. "Chip" Conyers and Carl Vaught, with whom I discussed many of the ideas in this book, passed away before I could adequately thank them for their important roles in my own intellectual, moral and spiritual development. Of all of these friends I owe a special debt of gratitude to Douglas Henry, Barry Harvey and John O'Callaghan. Most of what is written here was first discussed and argued through with them. And though I am quite sure that they do not agree with all that I have written here, I have certainly stolen more good ideas, illustrations and turns of phrase from them than I can count.

It is certainly the case that this collection of reflections would have never seen the light of day without the fine work of the InterVarsity Press staff. The anonymous reviewers offered superb suggestions. Former IVP editor Rodney Clapp convinced me that it should be a book, and Gary Deddo persevered with me when other editors would have let it slip into the abyss. Gary's keen editorial eye has made this a much better book. To both men I am immensely grateful. To my parents, Andy and Rachel Moore, and my in-laws, Ronald and Ann Harrell, I owe more than I can express.

I am most grateful for the love and support that comes from my extraordinary wife, Andrea, and our five children, Emily Anne, Benjamin, Hannah, Samuel and Andrew. And yet merely to say that I am grateful for them hardly does justice to the reality. Nothing much that happens in my life would be possible or valuable without Andrea. She is the love of my life, my constant companion, my best friend. And the journey with our children from their childhood through adolescence and toward maturity continues to be one of the greatest blessings of our lives. The hopes and dreams for the extraordinary politics expressed in this book are in a very real sense the hopes and dreams we have for our children. We hope they will know and contribute to that extraordinary politics that arises from the experience of God's grace and moves us beyond a culture of convenience and consumption and into the divine hospitality which is the pilgrim life of the people of God.

# 1

# INTRODUCTION

## The End of Convenient Stereotypes

WALKER PERCY'S 1971 NOVEL *Love in the Ruins* is set "in these dread latter days of the old violent beloved U.S.A. and of the Christ-forgetting Christ-haunted death-dealing Western world." Narrator Dr. Tom More begins with his delightfully disturbing description of life in the Paradise Estates suburb, just before the "end of the world." More tells us that

> the scientists, who are mostly liberal and unbelievers, and the businessmen, who are mostly conservative and Christian, live side by side in Paradise Estates. Though the two make much of their differences—one speaking of "outworn dogmas and creeds," the other of "atheism and immorality," etcetera etcetera—to tell the truth, I do not notice a great deal of difference between the two.

Here, according to More, "everyone gets along well." It is "a paradise indeed, an oasis of concord in a troubled land. For our beloved old U.S.A. is in a bad way. Americans have turned against each other; race against race, right against left, believer against heathen."[1]

---

[1]Walker Percy, *Love in the Ruins* (New York: Farrar, Strauss & Giroux, 1971), pp. 3, 15, 17.

In More's account, the Republicans, who had changed their name to the Christian Conservative Constitutional Party and even printed campaign buttons in support of their new CCCP, became the "Knothead Party" for "the most knotheaded political bungle of the century—which the conservatives, in the best tradition, turned to their own advantage, printing a million more buttons reading 'Knotheads for America.'" The Democrats became the new Left Party and also accepted a nickname, "LEFTPAPASANE," an acronym which stood for what the Left believed in: "Liberty, Equality, Fraternity, The Pill, Atheism, Pot, Anti-Pollution, Sex, Abortion Now, Euthanasia." Percy has his Dr. More observe: "The center did not hold. However, the Gross National Product continues to rise."[2]

Unlike that Dr. More, I do not believe that we are living at the "end of the world." In many parts of the United States and abroad, the illusion of an American paradise was shattered by the terrorist attacks of September 11, 2001. It is now a commonplace to observe that the world was changed forever and that we have now entered into a new age. On the contrary, the world did not fundamentally change that September morning, but it is true that we have come close to the end of an age which has defined our world and given meaning to our many endeavors. The age in question is modernity, that modern age in which free men and women have sought to produce political paradises. Both the religious and the irreligious act as if they know how to produce such a place, but frequently, like More's believers and unbelievers, there is not a "great deal of difference between the two."

This book is not about creating a new political paradise or recovering an old one. It is not about why "we can't all just get along" or how to find the true center amid the cacophony of political and moral extremes. It is not another book about religion and politics that announces whether it is really the Democrats or the Republicans who "speak for God." If we think that a political party (or a nation-state) can speak for God, we have already created an idol.

This book is about the peculiar state of affairs we find when Christians

---

[2]Ibid., pp. 17-18.

of various political inclinations begin to recognize that many of the political assumptions and commitments they have taken for granted neither can nor should be taken for granted any longer. It is about the challenge to faith and the practical idolatry which occurs when Christians assume that the language, concepts, habits and goals of democratic processes offer the best (or only) resources for solving the most pressing issues of our shared lives. It is about the surprising recognition of what democracy cannot do. It is about what happens after Christians discover the limits of Liberal democracy. These limits concern how we *talk*, *act* and *think* about politics—that is, the ordered life of the *polis*.

Christians exploring "the limits of Liberal democracy" might strike fear in the hearts of secularists, adherents of other faiths and even other Christians. Just what is meant by "the limits of Liberal democracy"? Visions of Margaret Atwood's *The Handmaid's Tale* may run through the mind's eye. Is this an attempt to undermine the separation of church and state? Use tax money for evangelism? Not only display, but also enforce, the Ten Commandments? Usher in a new theocratic government?

No. All of these questions and fears assume that *politics* is essentially about government or, more precisely, about *statecraft*, the art and skill of conducting the affairs of the nation-state. In the modern world it is often assumed that what is most important about politics can be reduced to statecraft. But *politics* refers to so much more than statecraft. One of the guiding assumptions of this book is that politics must be understood in a larger, more inclusive sense and must *not* be reduced to statecraft. Politics is about how we order our lives together in the *polis*, whether that is a city, a community or even a family. It is about how we live together, how we recognize and preserve that which is most important, how we cultivate friendships and educate our children, how we learn to think and talk about what kind of life really is the good life.

What is the good life? There are, of course, no easy answers to this most ancient of questions, but today most citizens of the United States (including most Christians) would point toward some combination of prosperity, security and personal well-being. "Personal well-being" is an amorphous catch-all for everything from physical and mental health to education and good manners, but prosperity and security are made possible by good government. Many believe that there is no good life without good government, and the only truly good government is democratic government. Woodrow Wilson famously took the United States into World War I in order "to make the world safe for democracy," and the contemporary "war on terror" is often described in precisely the same terms.

Commentators as diverse as Richard Rorty, Cornel West, Gertrude Himmelfarb and George Will have each argued that the individual who has been shaped and formed by democracy will not only be equipped to become the most mature and astute type of human being, he or she will also be equipped to form the most prosperous and just societies. In the words of George Will, statecraft is the model for soulcraft.[3]

But is democracy up to this challenge? Aren't there aspects of democracy that subtly transform or even corrupt our abilities and inclinations to become the kinds of people who are capable of seeing and loving the world as God would have us to? As far as statecraft goes, the Liberal nation-state is unmatched, and in the twentieth century, we have had ample opportunity to view the fascist and communist challenges brought against Liberal democracy. As statecraft, Liberal democracy works pretty well. But what kinds of *souls* does democracy form? More specifically, is the democracy which is principally committed to the autonomy of the individual and the expansion of personal liberty (i.e., Liberal democracy) capable of forming the souls of Christians who believe that "he who loves his life loses it, and he who hates his life in this world will keep it to life eternal" (John 12:25)? Can Liberal democracy secure physical security and financial prosperity for us Christians without subtly capturing our highest allegiances and quietly transforming our assumptions about what counts as happiness and success?

One of my operating assumptions is that Liberal political discourse is designed for those sociocultural contexts in which our expectations for human flourishing are at their lowest. This means that the tendency of the culture of Enlightenment Liberalism, which has steadily exported its

---

[3]George Will, *Statecraft as Soulcraft: What Government Does* (New York: Simon and Schuster, 1983); Richard Rorty, *Achieving Our Country* (Cambridge, Mass.: Harvard University Press, 1998); Cornel West, *Democracy Matters* (New York: Penguin, 2004); Gertrude Himmelfarb, *One Nation, Two Cultures* (New York: Knopf, 1999), p. 83.

principles, vocabularies and methodologies from the necessarily public sphere of statecraft (where it works, more or less, pretty well) into almost every other sphere of our daily lives (where it is far less successful), must be checked and can only be checked by communities that have both constituting narratives and sustaining practices strong enough to challenge the linguistic and imaginative hegemony of Liberal democracy.

This volume explores the consequences for religion and politics when believers begin to doubt that it is always possible to be both a good Christian and a good American. Most American Christians have never had cause to suspect a tension between these cherished dual identities. Most cannot imagine betraying either one. But the passing of modernity presents new challenges for American Christians, as more Christians are forced to recognize that in a world with fewer and fewer Christians, democratic faith also makes ever more exclusive demands. But the end of the Christian love affair with democracy leaves a gaping whole. For most Christians it cannot be filled with either "theocracy" or an impulse toward sectarian retreat. And summoning age-old admonitions on behalf of the culture wars for a "Christian America" looks less and less persuasive with every passing day.

In the conclusion to *After Virtue*, Alasdair MacIntyre reflects on the crucial turning point at the end of the Roman Empire "when men and women of good will turned aside from the task of shoring up the Roman *imperium* and ceased to identify the continuation of civility and moral community with the maintenance of that *imperium*." According to MacIntyre, they found themselves constructing "new forms of community within which the moral life could be sustained so that both morality and civility might survive the coming age of barbarism and darkness." MacIntyre believes "that for some time now we too have reached that turning point. What matters at this stage is the construction of local forms of community within which civility and the intellectual and moral life can be sustained through the new dark ages which are already upon us."[4]

This book is first and foremost an inquiry into what counts as "politics," and what relevance life in the Christian community might have both for

---

[4]Alasdair MacIntyre, *After Virtue*, 2nd ed. (Notre Dame, Ind.: University of Notre Dame Press, 1984), p. 263.

how we think about this broader, more expansive understanding of politics, and how we create forms of Christian community which can sustain the intellectual and moral life. And in that sense the book is entirely about learning to think about politics in a different and more distinctly Christian manner. But the distinctly Christian manner has virtually nothing to do with choosing between the conflicting Democratic and Republican proposals for statecraft. While I am not completely cynical on this score, I'm inclined to agree with Tom More: there is not a "great deal of difference between the two." What was true for MacIntyre's Roman Christians is true for American Christians as well. We must be prepared to cease to identify the continuation of civility and moral community with the imperium that has been Liberal democracy and turn our attention toward the cultivation of new forms of community.

But why should one think that we are in an analogous historical situation? Why believe that modernity is coming to an end or that the glorious experiment called the Enlightenment has finally begun to wane?

What is the Enlightenment? That is no small question, and it has puzzled thoughtful observers of society and culture from Immanuel Kant to Michel Foucault and beyond. Historically, the period of time known as the Enlightenment began about three hundred years ago—this epoch after the "Dark Ages" through the birth pangs of the Renaissance, when the freedoms afforded by science, rationality and individualism emerged from the bondage allegedly brought on by superstition, dogma and the hierarchical authorities of the Middle Ages. The Enlightenment ushered us into the modern world. It was for this reason that Kant thought of the Enlightenment as giving birth to the maturity of the human spirit. This maturity was all about autonomy and individualism, and manifested itself in subject-centered rationality and in Liberal democracy, that form of government which traded the divine rights of kings and popes for the inalienable rights of all "men"—who were proclaimed to be created equal and endowed by their Creator with these rights. Unfortunately, not even all the "men" (to say nothing of the women) were ever recognized as equal, as far more than half the population was systematically alienated from these inalienable rights.

In recent years, however, the Enlightenment legacy has fallen on hard times, as more and more observers have recognized that the Enlightenment project was not merely unfinished but perhaps unfinishable. In the words of MacIntyre, the Enlightenment project of justifying morality "had to fail" given its contradictory impulses and aspirations.[5] The spirit that animated the Enlightenment project is clearly alive, but not well. In fact, a mindset which prized openness and tolerance above all other virtues began to appear closed to competing visions and vigorously intolerant of rival interpretations. These rival interpretations have produced a conflict within modernity.

Philosophers typically describe modernity in epistemological terms. The modern human being has different standards for knowledge and knows and evaluates the world in new ways. However, as it has unfolded these past three centuries, modernity's epistemological innovations have been tied in many and unexpected ways to the rise and development of the nation-state. More precisely, modern knowing has been superseded and incorporated by the hegemony of the state.[6] (Later I demonstrate how Immanuel Kant's essay "What Is Enlightenment?" illustrates particularly well the subtle transformation of epistemology by the state.) The modern age is in fact the age of the nation-state. To be modern is to be an individual in just such a nation-state. By implication, to be postmodern is, at the most fundamental level, to refuse to accept the state as the most fundamental reality for the human being, and this obviously has implications for epistemology.

During the fall and winter of 1996 and 1997, two events played out in the United States that illustrated the bankruptcy of the conventional wisdom about religion and politics. The two events were both described in the national media as confusing the very categories used to make sense of the national conversation on religion and public life. The events in question were the published symposium (and its response) on the judicial usurpation of politics at the Institute on Religion and Public Life, and the controversial hiring of a young priest at the University of

---

[5]Ibid., pp. 51-61.
[6]"Superseded and incorporated" is not quite right. It is actually a process of transformation whereby one developmental stage is overcome but preserved in a new key. Hegel describes this as *Aufhebung*, usually and inadequately translated as "sublimation."

Notre Dame. Critics of both actions lodged strong protests on both procedural and substantial grounds. Both issues arose out of a refusal to accept democracy as the most fundamental reality for the flourishing of human life.

One can point to other examples of current events or recent programs that similarly demonstrate the inadequacy of the discourse of Enlightenment Liberalism to come to terms with these phenomena. However, I begin with the two already-mentioned items because the cast of characters and the issues underlying these events overlap in so many interesting and ironic ways. While it might not be immediately obvious why evangelicals and other Protestants (to say nothing of secularists) should care about two largely Catholic events, it will become clear that the tension between Christian and democratic faith arises from the democratic demand for accommodation, and this deep challenge of accommodationism affects Catholic and Protestant alike.

This book grows out of an earlier essay, "The End of Convenient Stereotypes: How the *First Things* and Baxter Controversies Inaugurate Extraordinary Politics," originally published in *Pro Ecclesia* (winter 1998) and republished by Spence Publishing in a separate collection.[7] In that essay I misunderstood the nature of the project I was working on. At the time, I thought that the two events rendered the conventional labels *liberal* and *conservative* problematic for contemporary Liberal democracy. Surely that much was true, though, as was frequently mentioned to me, it was true and trivial. In that essay I hinted at an "extraordinary politics" I did not fully understand. This book attempts to express my new understanding of extraordinary politics, the radical politics of an alternative *polis*—the church.

The phrase *extraordinary politics* is borrowed from Thomas Kuhn's notion of "extraordinary science." In Kuhn's landmark *The Structure of Scientific Revolutions*, he distinguishes between "normal science" and "extraordinary science."[8] Normal science is the "puzzle-solving" enterprise which characterizes scientific research during periods of relative agreement about

---

[7]*The End of Democracy II*, ed. Mitchell S. Muncy (Dallas: Spence Publishing, 1999).
[8]Thomas Kuhn, *The Structure of Scientific Revolutions*, 3rd ed. (Chicago: University of Chicago Press, 1996).

fundamental assumptions and procedural methodologies. There are always unanswered questions (puzzles that cannot be solved) in scientific research, but as long as these questions are at the margins of inquiry, the dominant paradigm for research remains unchallenged. However, if the unanswered questions move to the center of inquiry, some scientists will revise or abandon fundamental assumptions, creating alternative paradigms for understanding the subject at hand. Extraordinary science occurs when there are competing paradigms for understanding the most basic questions in the field. Rival paradigms cannot be evaluated merely on the basis of scientific data because the assumptions dictate what counts as data and how it is to be understood. Kuhn compared the adoption of a new paradigm to a political revolution or a religious conversion. I have chosen the phrase *extraordinary politics* to refer to that politics which challenges the dominant paradigm of Liberal democracy. In the course of these reflections I return to and expand upon Kuhn's metaphor.

The Baxter and *First Things* controversies are emblematic of a different problem. They illustrate anew, rather than "inaugurate," the age-old tension between the Christian and the state—specifically, the modern nation-state of the United States of America. The *First Things* symposium was not really about the "end of democracy." It was about the end of our Christian love affair with democracy. The Baxter controversy at Notre Dame was not merely about faculty hiring, departmental integrity or "democratic process." It was about a particular Christian commitment abrogating a certain infatuation with democracy and democratic procedure. Both cases are problematic and, as numerous critics have pointed out, represent "dangerous precedents." But both cases stand above all else as a rejection of the Kantian Liberalism of John Rawls, which is itself representative of the modern democratic nation-state. And Christians in the United States, like many others, have been enthralled by this nation-state.

I see this book as an attempt to contribute to reflection on what William Cavanaugh has called "Christian practice which escapes the thrall of the State."[9] (I have used Cavanaugh's insightful phrase throughout these reflections.) My intention is to think Christianly about being a Christian

---

[9]William T. Cavanaugh, " 'A Fire Strong Enough to Consume the House': The Wars of Religion and the Rise of the State," *Modern Theology* 11, no. 4 (1995): 409.

in a participatory democracy after a very bloody twentieth century. My intention is to reflect on how Christians should begin to think about faith, culture and politics once we have given up our illusions about how Christendom will flourish in a world made safe for democracy. And this brings me back to Walker Percy.

In one of Percy's insightful descriptions of his beloved New Orleans, he chronicles its virtues and vices, its opportunities and inadequacies. Though he wrote almost four decades prior to the tragedy of Hurricane Katrina and its aftermath, what Percy wrote in 1968 remains true in 2008. Amid its many troubles, Percy notes, "and yet New Orleans can point to this or to that which usually confirms the seeds of destruction and offers the hope of redemption. Here resides the best hope and the worst risk." Percy comes back and makes the point explicitly: "There is nearly always an *and yet*."[10]

Politics on the model of Enlightenment Liberalism has usually assumed that one's best hope consists in foreclosing on one's worst risk. Specifically, that means keeping religious insights, convictions and conversations out of the public square. From the Enlightenment's point of view, religion simply represents too great a risk. There is much truth in that sentiment. Religious faith is dangerous.

*And yet.* The Enlightenment never did keep religion out of the public square; it merely substituted a new religion, a ersatz religion based on a very particular type of reason and a special understanding of this reason's passion—in the end, not too different from traditional religion—as the lingua franca of enlightened Liberal political discourse. Tolerance and "openness" became the new cardinal virtues, so long as one was neither tolerant nor open to the intolerant closed-mindedness of certain worldviews and life plans. This Liberal political discourse has not lost its privileged status in the contemporary culture, but it has become increasingly difficult to avert our eyes from these curious ironies and quaint incoherences. I want to tell part of the story of how this came to be and of what happens next. The waning of Enlightenment Liberalism presents the Christian church with exciting new possibilities for "overcoming the thrall of the State."

---

[10]Walker Percy, "New Orleans Mon Amour," in *Signposts in a Strange Land*, ed. Patrick Samway (New York: Noonday Press, 1991), p. 17.

One of the difficulties in writing a book such as this one is that I must employ the very terminology my thesis calls into question. Toward these ends, a word of clarification is in order. As is common, when I speak of (capital *L*) *Liberalism* (or *Enlightenment Liberalism*), I am referring to the grand Western Liberal tradition that professes to affirm "value neutrality" and regards the autonomy of the individual as not only an intrinsic good which democratic government can guarantee but also as a foundational good which trumps all other values. It is this grand tradition (which always affirms that it is not a "tradition," strictly speaking) which has secured religious liberty but which is increasingly accused of privatizing (and trivializing) religion in the process. The heroes of Liberalism include John Locke, Immanuel Kant, John Stuart Mill and John Rawls. (In this book I do not treat the complex Western Conservative tradition that is historically Royalist in orientation and rejected the sovereignty of the individual while privileging the role of institutions and custom. Edmund Burke is the finest representative of political Conservatism.)

When I speak of (lower case *l*) *liberalism,* I am referring to the recent political tradition which values comprehensive government in the modern welfare state. Likewise, the term (lower case *c*) *conservative* refers to the corresponding tradition of minimalist government. The complicated question of *neo-conservative* identity is addressed later. All three (liberals, conservatives and neo-conservatives) participate in the larger Enlightenment Liberal culture. On this construal it should be obvious that even conservative politicians like Margaret Thatcher and Ronald Reagan are Liberals in the larger, more comprehensive sense; indeed, most modern Americans are Liberals, or recovering Liberals (myself included), given our virtually ubiquitous commitment to individual freedom and the sovereignty of personal rights. This is also why it is hard for Christians to recognize the tacit tensions between their Christian and democratic faiths.

Political Liberalism can be understood as operating from three crucial assumptions: (1) politics is reducible to statecraft; (2) the objective (*telos* or goal) of Liberal politics is to fashion a statecraft (or create a government) which guarantees security while maximizing individual liberty; and (3) political conversation and inquiry must focus on the means or procedure for achieving these goals. These assumptions can lead to the unpleasant consequence of convincing their practitioners that they do not have to argue for the superiority of the alleged agreed-upon goal. What Richard Rorty calls the "priority of democracy to philosophy" is the assertion that democratic Liberalism does not "need" philosophical justification.[11] Frequently Enlightenment Liberals do not even *feel* (and I do want to emphasize the emotive connotations) the need to argue for a particular procedure. Debate simply focuses on whether "proper" procedure was followed. This conversation ("was everything done properly?") avoids the difficult question "What should we be doing?" for the self-deceptive question "How should we be doing it?"

Typically, when (we) Liberals do talk about ends, we want to talk about the "validity" of these ends. Of course, *validity* is a formal or structural, not a material, category, and therefore it is a category that is entirely congenial to our Liberal preoccupation with procedure. I follow the lead of philosophers like Hans-Georg Gadamer who have reminded us that while our truths are indeed a product of our methods, following the established method is no guarantee of arriving at the Truth.[12]

As already noted, some Liberals today choose to speak of Liberalism as a tradition. This, to me, seems entirely correct and very helpful. Liberalism, in so many respects, is a good and worthy "ism." Understood as a tradition, it is one of the most vibrant and hopeful models for the political discourse of statecraft. Of course, it must be recognized that Liberals have almost always wanted to avoid having Liberalism characterized as a tradition, and for good reason. When Liberalism is viewed as one option competing among others, it loses its most effective weapon: it forfeits its prized status as the "neutral" position committed only to those propositions that can be demonstrated as true. As a tradition, gone are its claims that it has no agenda, no grounding assumptions and no sacred authorities; gone is the cherished belief that it is only concerned with procedure and fairness and justice; and gone is the convenient and comforting belief that keeps all

---

[11]Richard Rorty, "The Priority of Democracy to Philosophy," *Objectivity, Relativism, and Truth* (Cambridge: Cambridge University Press, 1991).
[12]Hans-Georg Gadamer, *Truth and Method*, 2nd ed., trans. Joel Weinsheimer and Donald G. Marshall (New York: Continuum, 1991).

this scandalous particularity under rap.

After this introductory chapter, the second chapter presents the story of the 1996 *First Things* symposium on "The End of Democracy?" and the response of its critics. I begin with a narrative overview of each of the original essays. After turning to the relevant background (some brief history of the journal and its controversial founder, Richard John Neuhaus), I focus on the extraordinary response to the controversy. The *First Things* symposium calls into question traditional sensibilities about how conservative Christians relate to democracy.

The third chapter introduces Michael Baxter and the controversy surrounding his 1996 appointment at the University of Notre Dame. The chapter's structure is the same as chapter two: narrative, background and response to the controversy. The narrative contains a brief history of Baxter's hire, the theology department's protest and the Notre Dame faculty senate's investigation. By way of background, I summarize Baxter's critique of the Americanist tradition and the theology department's embodiment of that tradition. The chapter concludes with a discussion of the varied responses to Baxter's appointment. The Baxter controversy calls into question traditional sensibilities about how liberal Christians relate to democracy.

Chapter four addresses why these two events ought to be viewed together and why they are significant both for non-Catholics and secularists. The ambiguity surrounding the principal figures is mirrored in their different struggles with the notion of natural law. Here we see operating rival versions of the relationship that natural law plays between politics and faith. Christian postmodernists (like Baxter and Stanley Hauerwas) are tempted to redescribe (and sometimes abandon) appeals to natural law in favor of a robust Christian particularism. Christian modernists (like Neuhaus) who have previously been tempted to use Enlightenment Liberalism (understood as neoconservative politics and economics) to support natural law now find themselves to be "reluctant particularists" (though this term is problematic as we shall see).

Chapter five begins with a response to a criticism of my thesis raised by Neuhaus. Neuhaus rejected my construal of Gertrude Himmelfarb's position and wants "to view Himmelfarb and people of like mind as allies." I argue that neo-conservatives like Himmelfarb and Norman Podhoretz share three crucial beliefs with liberals like Richard Rorty that place them at odds with Christians like Neuhaus. First, they understand religion in principally functional or utilitarian terms. Second, they believe that religion as anything other than a functional impulse (for instance, a public and political practice) is a "conversation-stopper." Third, and most important, they affirm Rorty's notion of "the priority of democracy to philosophy," the belief that one's commitments to democracy not only substantially inform all inquiry into the nature of human flourishing but also that democracy trumps any truth claims which might call democracy into question—faithfulness to Christ included. This commitment exemplifies the reduction of politics to statecraft.

Chapter six seeks to explain this difficult phrase "the reduction of politics to statecraft." The fundamental issue here is the nature of human maturity. Because the Christian *polis* understands what it means to be a mature human being uniquely, it produces a different sort of person and a different guiding conception of politics than Liberal democracy. To argue for this conclusion, I offer a brief genealogy of the transformation of maturity as it is found in Thomas Hobbes, Immanuel Kant and Max Weber before turning to the effects of this transformation on our contemporary situation. The chapter concludes with a demonstration of how the reduction of politics to statecraft transforms a social institution such as marriage through the importation of a certain set of assumptions, vocabularies and procedures.

Chapter seven explores how the extraordinary politics of an alternative *polis* (the church) engages the larger culture of convenient consumption. Here I argue that alternative virtues and practices can offer a compelling response to those dilemmas presented to us today in the culture of death—abortion, euthanasia and capital punishment. Inspired and enabled by the gospel of life, we can begin to learn how to escape the thrall of the state.

The concluding chapter offers a concrete example of extraordinary politics through a discussion of the practice of hospitality. In this chapter I demonstrate that hospitality is a more compelling political practice than tolerance, the foundational practice of Enlightenment Liberalism. Here I make a brief case for hospitality by offering two suggestions. First, hospitality, considered in a general, nonreligious way as a community-forming practice, has a chance of succeeding where tolerance falters. Second, Christians have a particular incentive to exercise hospitality because we recognize that this practice takes its bearings from divine action.

By focusing on hospitality and extraordinary politics, I hope to help Christians rise above the hegemonic conception of politics given to us by the modern state. Constantine made the Roman Empire safe for Christianity, and Christians spent the next millennium-and-a-half trying to turn Christian ideals into effective statecraft. That day is over. If the end of Constantianism means the end of Christians thinking that we control the state and the culture, it also means the end of letting the state control how we think about the ordered life of the *polis*. It means rejecting the state's claim on our ultimate allegiance.

I did not write this book as an essay against democratic statecraft or even against Enlightenment Liberalism writ large. As I have already noted, I am, in many senses, a Liberal, and my education has been a product of the Enlightenment. Furthermore, I value participatory democracy, and with all our nation's problems (and they are legion), I believe we must recognize that many of us share and enjoy many freedoms, prosperities and opportunities not available in other parts of the world. This must not be taken for granted. Unfortunately, for those of us who are Christians, our enjoyment of these freedoms has frequently led us to think about *freedom* and *prosperity* in ways not consistent with our faith. And to the extent that we have assumed that the categories of thought and action produced by Enlightenment Liberalism are one and the same as those of our faith, we have chosen the cheerful delusion of prosperity. At the end of our convenient stereotypes, this becomes a luxury we can no longer afford.

# 2

# THE END OF
# DEMOCRACY?

### The *First Things* Symposium and Its Critics

*FIRST THINGS* IS THE MONTHLY PUBLICATION of the Institute on
Religion and Public Life in New York City. It has become one of the most
visible national journals of opinion, and it is perhaps the most widely read
monthly publication on religion and politics. Despite the fact that it presents a wide range of opinions in its feature articles, *First Things* is a decid-
edly conservative publication, by most standards. Its editorials, opinion
essays and reviews echo largely conservative themes, and founding editor
Richard John Neuhaus's monthly column, "The Public Square," is an
often rambunctious, satirical commentary on current publications and hap-
penings, and on what he takes to be liberalism's self-delusory seriousness.

In its November 1996 issue *First Things* published a symposium titled
"The End of Democracy? The Judicial Usurpation of Politics."[1] The sym-

---

[1]*First Things* 67 (November 1996): 18-42. Parenthetical references in this chapter are to this issue
of *First Things*.

posium included articles by Russell Hittinger, Robert Bork, Hadley
Arkes, Charles Colson and Robert George, and an introductory editorial
authored by Neuhaus. The symposium investigated the question of
whether the consent of the governed is compromised or even forfeited by
a judiciary which has "in effect declared that the most important questions about how we ought to order our life together are outside the pur-
view of 'the things of [the citizenry's] knowledge.' " What were the implications of the judiciary's repeated foreclosing on the process of legislative
debate and decision through the creation of previously unrecognized constitutional rights? Do such actions call into question "the legitimacy of the
regime"? In the months that followed, a firestorm of more than two hundred essays, documents, responses, and published letters and editorials
flooded the national media seeking to answer, repudiate or confirm the
assertions of the symposiasts.[2] More than a decade after the symposium,
it still generates comment in national publications.

It was Neuhaus's introduction to the symposium that became the light-
ning rod attracting the most media attention. It was the most often (and
frequently the *only*) quoted document of any of the essays published in the
symposium. Neuhaus noted that this symposium was an "extension" of a
May 1996 *First Things* editorial, "The Ninth Circuit's Fatal Overreach."
The "overreach" in question was the Ninth Circuit's decision to overturn
a Washington State law banning physician-assisted suicide on the grounds
that the Constitution guarantees a "liberty right" to assisted suicide. The
May editorial suggested that if "the Supreme Court upholds the Ninth
Circuit, the battle over abortion would likely be transformed into near
unconditional warfare against the arrogance of the courts that short-
circuit democratic deliberation by the imposition of their moral (or grossly
immoral) dictates."[3]

Conservative political commentators and politicians have long lamented
judicial activism, and many viewed this symposium as simply one more
refrain of this familiar conservative chorus. The fact that the November
symposium appeared just two months prior to the scheduled oral argu-

---

[2]A complete bibliography of items published before July 1997 can be found in *The End of Democracy?*
*The Judicial Usurpation of Politics*, ed. Richard John Neuhaus (Dallas: Spence Publishing, 1997).
[3]"The Ninth Circuit's Fatal Overreach," *First Things* 63 (May 1996): 13.

ments on two physician-assisted suicide cases before the Supreme Court *(Compassion in Dying v. Washington* and *Quill v. Vacco)* was lost on no one. But the *First Things* symposium addressed more than the judicial exuberance of the Court. Almost all of the conservative critics who would later protest the *First Things* publication cited their agreement with the call for judicial restraint. What made this symposium unique (and raised the ire of so much of the conservative establishment) was the inference the symposiasts drew: within the judicial usurpation of politics lay the potential loss of the consent of the governed. To *First Things*, this meant that the American experiment in democracy was in jeopardy of failure.

Neuhaus did not mince words in his introduction. He explained that the question before this symposium was "whether we have reached or are reaching the point where conscientious citizens can no longer give moral assent to the existing regime" (p. 18). While acknowledging that the editors were prepared that some would see the publication of this symposium as "irresponsibly provocative and even alarmist," he noted that, in its recent jurisprudence, it was the Supreme Court itself that had tied its legitimacy to the reception of its judgments on controversial moral questions like abortion. According to Neuhaus, by the Supreme Court's own formulation, the question of legitimacy was on the table. Furthermore, it could not but be evaluated in light of those principles and truths affirmed by the populace. Moreover, "[a]mong the most elementary principles of Western Civilization is the truth that laws which violate the moral law are null and void and must in conscience be disobeyed" (p. 19). Martin Luther King Jr. and Pope John Paul II were cited as exemplars who had invoked this principle.

But even these comments might have been overlooked had not Neuhaus drawn a comparison to the atrocities committed under German National Socialism. This reference drew the most vitriolic response of the critics. After noting that Robert George's use of John Paul II's *Evangelium Vitae* reflected the pope's own allusion to Pius XI's *Mit Brennender Sorge* (*With Burning Concern*, which focused on the escalating dangers of the Third Reich), Neuhaus wrote these words: "America is not and, please God, will never become Nazi Germany, but it is only blind hubris that denies it can happen here and, in peculiarly American ways, may be happening here" (p. 19). Despite the fact that this statement, framed by an allusion to two popes, was a *denial* that the United States was in a similar position as Nazi Germany, it was enough to raise the rafters.

The first essay in the symposium, "Our Judicial Oligarchy" by Robert Bork, was also philosophically and religiously the weakest and the least connected with the more substantial themes of the symposium. Bork summarized recent Court decisions and made his familiar argument that the Court has chosen to make law in accordance with its current political and cultural fashion and not interpret law according to the Constitution. It was no surprise to discover in the January 1997 issue of *First Things* a letter from Bork reiterating the narrow scope of his own contribution to the symposium and distancing himself from the rest of the contributors.

Russell Hittinger, Warren Professor of Catholic Studies and Research Professor of Law at the University of Tulsa, turned explicitly to the question of the "legitimacy" of the Court in his contribution, "A Crisis of Legitimacy." It is important to remember, as noted in Neuhaus's introduction, that in 1992 it was the Supreme Court itself which had raised the specter of its "legitimacy" in its decision in *Planned Parenthood v. Casey*. The relevant remarks from that decision are worth noting again (as Neuhaus also quotes in his own analysis, "The Anatomy of a Controversy"). In *Casey*, the Court affirmed that

> like the character of an individual, the legitimacy of the Court must be earned over time. So, indeed, must the character of a Nation of people who aspire to live according to the rule of law. Their belief in themselves as such a people is not readily separable from their understanding of the Court invested with the authority to decide their constitutional cases and speak before all others for their constitutional ideals. If the Court's legitimacy should be undermined, then, so would the country be in its very ability to see itself through its constitutional ideals. The Court's concern with legitimacy is not for the sake of the Court but for the sake of the Nation to which it is responsible.[4]

Hittinger locates his comments in response to this "crisis of legitimacy"—

---

[4]*Planned Parenthood v. Casey*, quoted in Richard John Neuhaus, "Anatomy of a Controversy," *The End of Democracy* (Dallas: Spence Publishing, 1997), p. 240.

a crisis brought about by the Court's assertion that "its case law be given the obedience due to the Constitution"—even obedience to those laws that govern the making of other laws and that many citizens view as damaging the common good. According to Hittinger, such foundational laws are laws "(1) that deny protection to the weak and vulnerable, especially in matters of life and death, and (2) that systematically remove the legal and political ability of the people to redress the situation." Hittinger concludes, "A polity that creates and upholds such laws is unworthy of loyalty" (p. 26).

Hittinger proceeded by summarizing and reviewing those recent decisions that have called into question the moral and religious motivations of certain pieces of enacted legislation. Though "it is late in the day, and our options have dwindled," according to Hittinger, the possibility for reform in the judiciary still exists. He suggested three steps necessary for reform: (1) the people, through elected representatives, "must withdraw whatever tacit consent has been given to the new constitutional order"; (2) moral issues should not be "isolated from the broader constitutional crisis"; (3) the Court's "motivational analysis" must be addressed explicitly. Hittinger's essay concluded with these words:

> Unless the elected representatives of the people can compel the Court to refrain from invalidating political activity merely on the basis of the citizens' moral or religious motivation, the task of reform is blocked. Should that continue, the option remaining to right reason is the one traditionally used against despotic rule: civil disobedience. (p. 29)

This was the sort of language that fueled the controversy. A heretofore calm, conservative journal was sounding an alarm. Despotic rule? Civil disobedience? Even William J. Bennett remarked that this symposium reminded him of his "1960s graduate school days."[5] The rhetoric may be fiery, but it is important to note carefully what Hittinger was suggesting: that there are democratic avenues which like-minded citizens should pursue. The call to civil disobedience only arises in the context of a loss of those properly democratic options.

---

[5]William J. Bennett, "End of Democracy? A Discussion Continued," *First Things* 69 (January 1997): 19.

The third contribution, "A Culture Corrupted," was offered by Hadley Arkes, Edward Ney Professor of Jurisprudence and American Institutions at Amherst College. Arkes argued that recent judicial decisions were transforming the national culture in such a way as to silence the articulation, and limit severely the perpetuation, of traditional moral and religious beliefs. Arkes used the Court's decision in *Romer v. Evans* as an example.

In *Romer v. Evans* the Court overturned a Colorado law which would have prohibited that legislature from making laws that viewed sexual orientation as a category for nondiscrimination. Interpreting "Amendment 2" of the Colorado law proved to be problematic. Those opposing the amendment believed that it denied recourse under law to Colorado citizens who believed they were discriminated against because of their sexual orientation. Those in support of the amendment believed it merely protected those Colorado citizens who held moral objections to homosexuality from being legally coerced to hire or otherwise engage in business with individuals who practiced a homosexual lifestyle. The amendment passed by statewide referendum in 1992 but was declared unconstitutional by the Supreme Court in 1996.

The Court ruled that the Colorado law was motivated by an "animus"—an irrational prejudice—against homosexuals. Hittinger had already addressed the difficulties surrounding jurisprudence based on "motivational analysis." Arkes followed the implications of this ruling. Despite over three millennia of reflection by the Court in the Judeo-Christian tradition, *Romer* implies that "the Supreme Court itself has declared that a moral objection to homosexuality is indefensible" (p. 32). From this position, it follows that those who defend a position which the Court has deemed indefensible (despite the religious precedent) invite legal action against them. According to Arkes,

> It is one thing to say, as the courts already have, that the moral precepts of Christianity and Judaism may not supply the premises of law in the secular state. It is quite another to say that people who take those precepts seriously may be enduring targets of litigation and legal sanction if they have the temerity to voice those precepts as their own and make them the grounds of their acts even in their private settings. (p. 33)

Arkes concluded his essay by noting that the great Enlightenment philosopher Jean-Jacques Rousseau

> had it right: that all of this simply came along with the ethic of modernity, as it was spread through the diffusion of the sciences and the arts. "We have all become doctors, and we have ceased being Christians." Whatever the cause, it should be plain now that something in the religious sensibility has been deadened. (p. 33)

Charles Colson, of Watergate fame and the present chairman of Prison Fellowship, submitted an essay titled "Kingdoms in Conflict" to the symposium. Here Colson surveyed the history of Christian understandings of the relation between believers and the state, beginning with the biblical record and moving on to Augustine, Aquinas, Calvin, John Knox, Dietrich Bonhoeffer and Martin Luther King Jr. Not all of these luminaries are agreed, of course, but according to Colson a clear mandate emerges which suggests that God requires Christians to respect the law until the law demands an allegiance reserved for God alone.

Colson's principal interest in this essay, however, lay in the notion of the "social contract" behind the doctrine of the consent of the governed. According to Colson the "pressing question" is whether the governed populace and judicial governors "still recognize the essence of the contract" (p. 36). Colson believes that one could call upon Enlightenment figures such as Locke and Jefferson to make the case that the terms of the contract have been broken. It seems to Colson, however, "only the Church in some corporate capacity, not the individual Christian, has the authority to answer the question of allegiance to the present regime" (p. 37). And if the church were to determine that the "government had violated its God-given mandate," a variety of options present themselves—modeled by Christians as diverse as those who signed the Barmen Declaration to those who organized the Underground Railroad to those who, like Boston pastor and "Tea Party" participant Jonathan Mayhew, chose revolution in the name of conscience. Colson, however, was explicit that he did not believe that civil disobedience, let alone revolution, was called for at this time. He affirms,

> We must continue for now to work relentlessly within the democratic process. Abhorring a confrontation, we should be engaged in a search for wis-

dom and a consensus to help us respond to the crisis of the time. Our discussion about the duty of Christians to the current American political
order must be conducted with care, in a manner that is formal rather than
intuitive, deliberative rather than spontaneous, regulative rather than pragmatic. Calmness and seriousness of demeanor is necessary both to prevent
the media dismissing us as fanatics and to prevent individuals from taking
matters into their own hands. (p. 38)

Passages such as this one were rarely (if ever) quoted by those who took
umbrage at the *First Things* symposium. Yet even this statement begins
with what some might read as an ominous "for now." Colson's conclusion
seems to confirm those suspicions:

We dare not at present despair of America and advocate open rebellion.
But we must—slowly, prayerfully, and with great deliberation and serious
debate—prepare for what the future seems likely to bring under a regime
in which the courts have usurped the democratic process by reckless exercise of naked power. (p. 38)

This was the kind of "showdown between church and state" that so many
feared.

The final contribution to the original symposium was made by Robert P.
George and was titled "The Tyrant State." George, McCormick Professor
of Jurisprudence at Princeton University, suggests that while there was
certainly much to celebrate in the American democratic experiment, there
was also much that should give the thoughtful observer reason to pause.
Setting himself against Liberal proceduralism, George argued that legitimacy involves more than mere procedure. Quoting John Paul II from the
encyclical *Evangelium Vitae,* George notes that "any regime, including a
democratic one, degenerates into what the Pope calls a 'tyrant state' when
its law exposes the weakest and most vulnerable members of the community—those most in need of the law's protection—to private lethal violence or other forms of oppression" (p. 40).

According to George (and following *Evangelium Vitae*), the legitimacy
of this, or any, government must be viewed within the context of the strug-
gle between "the culture of life" and "the culture of death." Democracy, as
such, is a means not an end, and any government that trivializes human life

forfeits its privileged status. It is not enough for one to be "personally opposed" to abortion but to acquiesce in the perpetuation of unjust laws. George's essay concluded with a call to "people of good will—of whatever religious faith" to ask themselves whether the present government was in fact becoming the "tyrant state" which John Paul II described.

I do not offer this summary of the contributions to the symposium because the arguments of the various essays contributed to the controversy which followed on the heels of the symposium. In large measure they did not. Most of the positive and negative responses focused solely on Neuhaus's introduction. It seems to me that had the various respondents focused on the arguments presented in the symposium, the controversy that followed would have been very different. When various commentators did venture to quote from one of the essays other than Neuhaus's introduction, they often either missed the point that was being made or took some phrase out of context as evidence of the "incendiary" rhetoric of *First Things*.

Furthermore, it seems important to note that the symposium did not (*pace* its critics) condone or even offer an analysis of the range of responses ("from noncompliance to resistance to civil disobedience to morally justified revolution") which conscientious citizens might employ when confronted with legal obligations they found to be morally suspect. Indeed, in an editorial titled "To Reclaim Our Democratic Heritage" (accompanying a collection of follow-up essays by William J. Bennett, Mary Ann Glendon, Midge Decter, John Leo and James Dobson) in the January 1997 issue of *First Things*, the editors were at pains to state explicitly their purposes and to guard their ideas from being misappropriated by the ever-expanding, anti-government, militia culture in the United States. Reiterating that none of the November essays asserted that the present government of the United States is in fact illegitimate, the editors emphasized that the recognition of "the displacement of a constitutional order by a regime that does not have, will not obtain, and cannot command the consent of the people" is an important step in inaugurating a national conversation designed to reclaim our democratic heritage. Near the end of the essay, the editors affirm:

The delusions of weekend revolutionaries should not set the boundaries of political discussion. Indeed, acquiescence in judicial usurpation, far from warding off extremism, would likely increase the number of Americans who believe there is no alternative to violent change. We therefore call for the vigorous pursuit of every peaceful and constitutional means to return our country to its democratic heritage, and to encourage its people to take up again what Professor Glendon calls the hard work of citizens rather than subjects.[6]

## From Whence Cometh the Revolution?

*First Things* began publication in March 1990. It had been preceded by a smaller, less-known but well-respected publication, *This World*. Despite the fact that this predecessor publication had been founded by Irving Kristol, the new *First Things* was never merely another "neoconservative" publication. In its initial editorial of its initial issue, the editors of *First Things* set forth their "editorial prejudices" by asserting that "*First Things* means, first, that the first thing to be said about public life is that public life is not the first thing."[7] For the editors this meant that "for the sake of both religion and public life, religion must be given the priority." The editors continue:

> While religion informs, enriches, and provides a moral foundation for public life, the chief purpose of religion is not to serve public life. Here we discover a necessary paradox. Religion that is captive to public life is of little public use. Indeed, such captivity produces politicized religion and religionized politics, and the result, as we know from bitter historical experience, is tragedy for both religion and public life.[8]

One of the refrains that kept appearing throughout the spring and summer of 1997 was that *First Things* was promoting some sort of "religionized politics" which was incompatible with American democracy. This accusation would be difficult to substantiate either in the symposium in itself or throughout the short history of the journal in general. The "tragedy" of politicized religion and religionized politics, as they put it, was never far from the journal's sight.

---

[6]"To Reclaim Our Democratic Heritage," *First Things* 69 (January 1997): 28.
[7]"First Things First," *First Things* 1 (March 1990): 7.
[8]Ibid.

The journal has, however, always been concerned with questions about the "legitimacy" of the American political order and the success of the American "experiment" in democracy. In that same initial editorial, the editors also assert:

> If the American experiment in representative democracy is not in conversation with biblical religion, it is not in conversation with what the overwhelming majority of Americans profess to believe is the source of morality. To the extent that our public discourse is perceived to be indifferent or hostile to the language of Jerusalem, our social and political order faces an ever deepening crisis of legitimacy.[9]

By the mid to late 1990s, that crisis had come to a head.

Richard John Neuhaus was until his death in 2009 the heart and soul of *First Things*. Not only its founder and editor-in-chief, he was the president of the Institute on Religion and Public Life. Described by *US News and World Report* as one of the thirty-two most significant American intellectuals, Neuhaus has been a principal player in the "culture wars," long before they were designated as such. For four decades Neuhaus has been a public figure and an articulate Christian spokesman. In a volume such as this about "the end of convenient stereotypes," the caricature-defying Neuhaus certainly qualifies as one of the principal actors.

In his contribution to the 1990s installment of the *Christian Century*'s How My Mind Has Changed series, Neuhaus notes that when he was twenty-three and attempting to situate himself in a changing world, he determined to be "in descending order of importance, religiously orthodox, culturally conservative, politically liberal, and economically pragmatic." In 1991 and 1997, Neuhaus could proclaim, "That quadrilateral still serves."[10] Of those four descriptions, it is of course the notion of his "political liberalism" which has changed the most over the years.

Neuhaus converted to Catholicism from his Lutheran faith in 1990. As a Lutheran pastor in the 1960s, he had not only been a vocal proponent of

---

[9]Ibid., p. 8.

[10]Richard John Neuhaus, "Religion and Public Life: The Continuing Conversation," in *How My Mind Has Changed*, ed. James M. Wall and David Heim (Grand Rapids: Eerdmans, 1991), p. 52; Richard John Neuhaus, American Journal of Jurisprudence Conference, University of Notre Dame, April 16, 1997.

civil rights, he had also vigorously opposed the Vietnam War. In 1969, he coauthored with Peter Berger the book *Movement and Revolution*, in which Neuhaus defended the radical position against Berger's conservative "reluctant activism." In the words of Gary Dorrien, "The fire-breathing proclamations were left to Neuhaus."[11] In his essay "The Thorough Revolutionary," Neuhaus cautions against "careless revolutionisms" while defending a revolutionary consciousness that recognizes "that the times have brought things to a head, [that] things cannot go on as they are."[12]

Neuhaus confesses that although it is "increasingly problematic to call [himself] a liberal,"[13] he is still an "authentic" liberal—one who protests the illiberalism of the contemporary left. Neuhaus's description of Richard Bernstein (of the *New York Times*, not of The New School for Social Research) is probably an apt description of Neuhaus himself. He is "a true liberal, which is to say he is a principled opponent of the illiberalism that today passes for liberalism in the worlds of journalism, entertainment, philanthropy, and education, both higher and lower. Which is to say that [he] is a neoconservative."[14]

The tensions, ambiguities and equivocations of all of these terms are at the heart of this present volume. For the moment, it is perhaps safest merely to say that in recent years Neuhaus has found his primary allies among those who argue for minimalist government and an originalist interpretation of the Constitution, and among those who argue against the constitutional right to abortion on demand and a similar right to euthanasia. And though he has become far more identified with traditionally conservative causes and agendas, clearly he has not lost this "revolutionary consciousness" that recognizes that "things cannot go on as they are."

## RESPONSE TO THE *FIRST THINGS* SYMPOSIUM

The response to the symposium was not long in coming. Gertrude Himmelfarb and Peter Berger resigned from the *First Things* editorial board,

---

[11]Gary Dorrien, *The Neoconservative Mind: Politics, Culture, and the War of Ideology* (Philadelphia: Temple University Press, 1993), p. 283.

[12]Peter Berger and Richard John Neuhaus, *Movement and Revolution* (Garden City, N.Y.: Anchor Books, 1970), p. 127.

[13]Neuhaus, "Religion and Public Life," p. 53.

[14]Richard John Neuhaus, "Rediscovering Liberalism," *First Things* 48 (December 1994): 76.

and Walter Berns resigned from the editorial advisory board. Despite the fact that (among others) *National Review* offered an editorial and the *Weekly Standard* devoted an entire article to the symposium immediately after it was published, it was Jacob Heilbrunn's cover article in the *New Republic* ("Neocon v. Theocon") which focused national attention on the symposium and delivered the new abbreviations of the hour.[15] Heilbrunn examined not just the symposium but also Himmelfarb's, Berger's and Bern's resignations. To Heilbrunn, the brouhaha at the Institute on Religion and Public Life was indicative of "the widening schism on the intellectual right."

Heilbrunn tells the story of the symposium and the subsequent resignations with an eye toward demonstrating how the Catholic, theologically oriented conservatives (the "theocons") at *First Things* edged out the largely Jewish, economically oriented neoconservatives (the "neocons") because the former (in concert with the Religious Right) have aspirations for a "Christian nation" that the latter can neither stomach nor understand.

Pointing to the rift in the Republican party over whether to lead in the 1996 election with social or economic conservatism (and ultimately doing neither with any discernible effect), Heilbrunn proclaims that these tensions are the inevitable result of the irreconcilable differences between the neocon's Straussian view of politics and the theocon's Thomistic Catholicism.

In truth Heilbrunn's essay was embarrassingly inaccurate. Most of his gaffes were enumerated in a published exchange between Robert George, Michael Novak and Heilbrunn in the February 3, 1997, issue of the *New Republic*.[16] For instance, though Heilbrunn pitted the debate as the Catholics against the Jews, he failed to recognize that of the five original symposiasts, there were two Protestants (Bork and Colson), two Catholics (Hittinger and George) and one Jew (Arkes). Furthermore, the "Christian nation" rhetoric of the Religious Right was noticeably absent from the original symposium. More importantly, Heilbrunn's explication of natural law, Leo Strauss, Thomas Aquinas, the Catholic theologian

---

[15]"First Things First," *National Review*, November 11, 1996, pp. 16-18; David Brooks, "The Right's Anti-American Temptation," *Weekly Standard*, November 11, 1996, pp. 23-26; Jacob Heilbrunn, "Neocon v. Theocon," *New Republic*, December 30, 1996, pp. 20-24.
[16]"Neocon v. Theocon: An Exchange," *New Republic*, February 3, 1997, pp. 28-29.

Germain Grisez, and the relationship between theological and political discourse in general left quite a lot to be desired. And yet Heilbrunn characterized this debate as a schism within conservatism, and most commentators followed his lead. In this regard most commentators misunderstood the symposium.

According to Heilbrunn (and in time others would concur), the *First Things* editors and Neuhaus were blind-sided by the reactions of the Jewish neocons. But this hardly seems to be the case. In the October 1996 issue of *First Things* (the issue immediately prior to the symposium), Neuhaus reviewed Ralph Reed's *Active Faith*. There Neuhaus laments that Reed does not understand "why so many Jews are so powerfully attached to the notion that, the more secular the society, the safer it is for Jews."[17] Moreover, in the same article, Neuhaus foreshadows what is to come the following month. According to Neuhaus, "Reed does less than justice, indeed he almost ignores, what may become the most flammable issue in our public life, namely, the usurpation of power by the judiciary." Neuhaus continues,

> As Ralph Reed surely knows, the great task in the months and years ahead is, if one may be permitted the awful words, to de-legalize and re-politicize the great questions that are properly political. This will not happen without a very sharp challenge to business as usual—a challenge that some will no doubt condemn as an insurrectionary revolt against "the law of the land" (meaning the latest dumb decision of the courts).[18]

These sorts of comments are further evidence of how Heilbrunn (and hosts of others) misunderstood the *First Things* symposium. This was not about a "widening schism on the intellectual right." Neuhaus understood the fragile nature of a coalition between the neocons and the theocons, and had his primary concern been one of maintaining that coalition, the symposium would not have existed. It would have been too great a risk. Furthermore, the conflict of conscience cannot be negotiated by a "business as usual" approach to politics (what Ralph Reed represented to Neuhaus). The solution, as now can be clearly seen, involved a challenge which

---

[17]Richard John Neuhaus, "Ralph Reed's Real Agenda," *First Things* 66 (October 1996): 43.
[18]Ibid., p. 45.

certainly was interpreted as an "insurrectionary revolt."

As noted earlier, in January 1997, *First Things* attempted to clarify matters and continue the discussion by offering a response to some of the early criticism, but this only fueled the debate in some quarters. January and February also saw a spate of articles from of the *Washington Post*, *Lingua Franca*, the *Chronicle of Higher Education*, *American Spectator*, *National Review* (again), *New Republic* (also again), *Crisis* and much more. Little, it seems, would be accomplished at this point by rehearsing the arguments and assessments of the many who responded to the symposium. In due course I will turn to several of the responses. Many of the more provocative essays were collected and published in a volume appropriately titled *The End of Democracy? The Celebrated* First Things *Debate with Arguments Pro and Con* (Spence Publishing, 1997). This volume also contains Neuhaus's own response to the respondents, "The Anatomy of a Controversy."

One set of responses bears further comment, however. In its February 1997 issue *Commentary* presented a symposium of its own titled "On the Future of Conservatism."[19] Many of the contributors did interpret the *First Things* challenge as the "insurrectionary revolt" previously described. This neo-conservative standard-bearing journal asked a collection of fifteen conservative intellectuals to respond to three issues: (1) the significance of the November 1996 general election (in which, despite the "Gingrich revolution" of 1994, the Republican majority in Congress dwindled and a Democratic president was reelected for the first time in half a century); (2) the divisions within conservatism: "In particular, what to your mind are the longer-term implications of the radicalizing mood revealed in the *First Things* symposium?"; and (3) conservatism's "mandate" in the days to come.[20] Most of the *Commentary* contributors repudiated the "incendiary" rhetoric of the original *First Things* symposium, and almost to a person the *Commentary* symposiasts lamented the damage done to national conservative causes and politics.

---

[19]"On the Future of Conservatism," *Commentary*, February 1997, pp. 14-43. Contributors to the *Commentary* symposium include Robert L. Bartley, Peter Berger, Walter Berns, William F. Buckley Jr., Midge Decter, David Frum, Francis Fukuyama, Mark Helprin, Gertrude Himmelfarb, William Kristol, Michael Novak, Norman Podhoretz, Irwin M. Stelzer, George Wiegel and Ruth R. Wisse.

[20]Ibid., p. 15.

Public discussion of both the original symposium and the many issues raised in response continued through 1997 and 1998. In the spring of 1999, Spence Publishing produced a second volume of reflections on the controversy, *The End of Democracy? II: A Crisis of Legitimacy*.[21] The volume contained ten essays, including four revised pieces originally presented one year after the publication of the original symposium at a Loyola University (New Orleans) Law School conference on the theme "Judicial Usurpation and the End of Democracy, Once Again." Of the original symposiasts, Neuhaus, Hittinger, Arkes and George were invited to respond to the criticisms and to reflect on the abiding questions. Joining them on the platform were three Louisiana law professors (John Kramer, Tulane; Isabel Medina, Loyola; and Paul Baier, Louisiana State University) who were to respond critically to the issues raised.

Though there was some great drama and posturing, the Loyola conference was disappointing in many respects, producing more smoke than heat—let alone light. The crucial issues raised by Hittinger, Arkes and George on judicial usurpation and the conscientious response of religious citizens were largely avoided in favor of discussing more general disagreements on abortion and the like.

And yet a failed attempt at dialogue and conversation is illustrative of a deeper insight which is relevant to the larger aims of this study. At Loyola, in hallway conversations during and after the conference, observers and participants (pro and con), could be seen shaking their heads and heard confessing that their interlocutors across the aisle "just don't get it." Surely this was and is the case for both sides. Though Neuhaus had argued persuasively that "the question is theological," the Louisiana liberal critics, like the conservative *Commentary* critics before them, failed to understand this essential point of view. Both groups of critics repeatedly failed to see that this was a theological problem. From the perspective of the critics (surely unintentionally echoing the words of Gertrude Himmelfarb), the issue was "really" just abortion or maybe some other collection of moral dilemmas which democracy had not yet solved. The issue could not have been theological (there are no theo-

---

[21]Mitchell S. Muncy, ed., *The End of Democracy? II: A Crisis of Legitimacy* (Dallas: Spence Publishing, 1999).

logical public issues)—and if it was, it had no business in the public square. "They just don't get it."

It is an old saw that politics makes strange bedfellows. The verbatim criticisms of showy Louisiana liberals and stodgy Manhattan neoconservatives are a case in point. It would not be the last.

# 3

## AMERICAN CATHOLICS TO THE RESCUE?

### Michael Baxter and the Notre Dame Theology Department

THE UNIVERSITY OF NOTRE DAME WAS FOUNDED by the priests of the Congregation of Holy Cross (CSC) in 1842. Though the order no longer exercises primary control of the institution, the CSC continues to maintain a prominent, if less visible, presence on campus. There are certain provisions within Notre Dame's bylaws that guarantee a connection to the order and the university's heritage. Among other provisions, such require that the president of Notre Dame shall be a priest of the CSC (of the Indiana province) and that, with regard to faculty hiring, the CSC shall constitute an affirmative action category at Notre Dame. (To hire a CSC priest, an academic department is given an additional faculty line, but the person must meet expected qualifications.)

Michael Baxter (b. 1955) was a priest of the Congregation of Holy Cross. During the spring academic term of 1996, Baxter applied for a position in the theology department at Notre Dame. Baxter's nomination was rejected by the appointments committee of the theology department. Then university president Edward A. Malloy, CSC, subsequently appointed Baxter to a visiting three-year position in the department against the wishes of the appointments committee.

During the fall 1996 academic term, the theology department's rejection of Baxter and his subsequent appointment by President Malloy were all the rage in conversation on the Notre Dame campus. The rationale behind both actions was far from clear, however. While some members of the theology department expressed dismay over Baxter's rejection, others defended the appointments committee's action on the substantial grounds that Baxter was not a qualified candidate. President Malloy clearly believed otherwise.

In a letter written July 24, 1996, to then theology department chair Lawrence Cunningham, Malloy emphasized that he intended Baxter's visiting appointment as a "compromise." Malloy gave the following reasons for his decision to give Baxter this visiting appointment: (1) The president is entrusted with the responsibility of ensuring that university statutes and bylaws are faithfully discharged. These statutes include "mak[ing] full use of the unique skills and dedication of the members of the Priests of Holy Cross" and "eagerly and openly" pursuing qualified CSC priest-scholars. Malloy felt that Michael Baxter was not eagerly pursued. (2) Recognizing that Baxter's dissertation director at Duke, Stanley Hauerwas, was not only a former member of the Notre Dame theology department but also a participant in "some of the more controversial discussions" within that department, Malloy felt that Baxter "was unfortunately connected, if only unconsciously, with certain disputes in the Department's history." (3) On the basis of a professional judgment about Baxter's "scholarly and teaching credentials in [Malloy's] own subfield of theological ethics," Malloy believed that Baxter's qualifications warranted the visiting appointment.

During the fall term, members of the theology department brought this situation to the attention of the Notre Dame community at large. Theology department critics of Malloy's action voiced first substantial and later procedural objections to Baxter's appointment. It was, of course, exclusively a matter between the administration, the department and the

candidate, but it quickly became a matter of campuswide, and later na-
tionwide, controversy.

As Alfred Freddoso of the philosophy department would later say, "Certain members of the [theology] department have vociferously urged the
rest of us on the faculty to treat their business as our business," and such
certainly seems to be the case. In the year's first issue of the left-of-center
independent newspaper *Common Sense,* Joseph Blenkinsopp (John A.
O'Brien Professor in the theology department) repudiated Malloy's tendency to make major policy decisions during the summer when many faculty "resist the temptation to enjoy the summer in the heart of rural Indiana." Without mentioning Baxter by name, Blenkinsopp reported how a
CSC priest with a Ph.D. from Duke University had applied for a position,
been rejected by the department and "unilaterally appointed" to a visiting
position. Noting that the Notre Dame department ranked twelfth nation-
ally, Blenkinsopp asserted, "It is therefore hardly one of those depressing
cases of a mediocre department rejecting an outstanding candidate."[1]

The case had already become a depressing one for most of those involved. On September 11, 1996, faculty senate vice chair (and member
of the theology department) Jean Porter reported to the senate and presented a resolution from the executive committee which expressed "grave
concern" over the manner in which the appointment was made. By way
of background information, Porter affirmed (in summary) that the theology department "did not consider [Baxter] qualified for an appointment and turned down the application."[2] Porter wanted the senate to
pass the resolution condemning the administration's action at their September meeting. Faculty senate member Robert G. Blakey, O'Neil Professor of Law, Notre Dame Law School, expressed that it would be inappropriate for the senate to act without looking into the matter further.
Porter protested that there was nothing else to know; she had relayed
the relevant facts of the matter to the body. After discussion the senate
appointed its academic affairs committee to investigate the matter in
order to see if there had been any improprieties of governance with respect to Baxter's appointment over the wishes of the theology appoint-

---

[1] Joseph Blenkinsopp, "The Summer of Our Discontent," *Common Sense* 11, no. 1 (1996): 1.
[2] Senate proceedings minutes, September 11, 1996.

ments committee and to report its findings to the senate. The senate did not question Malloy's prerogative to overrule or his ultimate responsibility in matters of faculty appointments.

The meeting closed on a note that foreshadowed the distrust and anger that was to come. Porter publicly asked Blakey if he was calling her integrity into question. Blakey said that he just wanted to get the facts of the matter but would give her the benefit of the doubt. Porter noted that she expected a public apology when these matters were settled.

In its November 7 meeting, the academic affairs committee presented its report along with a minority report authored by Blakey. Blakey alleged that there were grievous procedural violations because the academic affairs committee did not conduct a full and fair investigation. It neither heard testimony nor gathered evidence beyond assembling various correspondence. Blakey argued that it was improper for the senate to speak on matters about which it had not gathered adequate evidence. For its part, the senate accepted both the majority report and Blakey's dissenting view, and recommitted the academic affairs committee's report and resolution back to the committee for further reflection in light of an upcoming resolution by the theology department.

The committee found (contra Blakey) "no evidence that the Theology Department failed to observe its responsibility to give 'special consideration' to a CSC candidate" and "no justification either for President Malloy's unilateral decision to appoint or for the manner in which he appointed a CSC candidate to a faculty position." Noting that the president's action "harms the Theology Department and the University as a whole by undermining the well-established and beneficial model of rational collaboration that exists between a departmental faculty and the university's administration with regard to hiring decisions," the senate expressed "its strong disapproval of President Malloy's handling of the 'special relationship' and its strong disapproval of his decision to appoint a Visiting Professor." On December 3, 1996, the senate passed a resolution which affirmed that President Malloy's decision "seriously erodes the confidence that a faculty ought to have in a President." The resolution passed 29 to 5, with three abstentions.[3]

---

[3]Notre Dame Faculty Senate Resolution, December 3, 1996.

## Michael Baxter

A past graduate of the Notre Dame theology department (Master of Divinity, 1983), Michael Baxter received his doctorate in theological ethics at Duke University. While at Duke he received several awards, including the prestigious Charlotte W. Newcombe Doctoral Dissertation Fellowship. Before coming to Notre Dame, Baxter received a Visiting Research Fellowship at the Center for the Study of American Religion at Princeton University. Prior to returning to Notre Dame, Baxter had made numerous conference presentations and published in both theological and jurisprudence journals. He also served on the editorial board of the *American Journal of Jurisprudence*.

A pacifist, Baxter is also a proponent of the Catholic Worker movement begun by Dorothy Day and exemplified by Catholics everywhere who see themselves as seeking to curb the exploitative consequences of market-driven capitalism. In the 1980s, Baxter cofounded and later served as director of the Andre House of Hospitality for the homeless and poor, and the St. Joseph the Worker Job Service, both in Phoenix, Arizona. During his seminary years at Notre Dame, he had established the Center for Draft and Military Counseling. While at Duke, in the weeks before the First Gulf War, he counseled conscientious objectors in the United States military stationed in Germany.

Earlier it was stated that the *First Things* symposiasts were exploring the question of whether we "have reached or are reaching the point where conscientious citizens can no longer give moral assent to the existing regime." Baxter had already reached this point. In 1983, he was arrested and later convicted in a federal court for an antinuclear arms protest at the Davis-Monthan Air Force Base near Tucson, Arizona. The conviction, which Baxter refers to as "one of our nation's highest honors," brought a sentence of two years probation and two hundred hours of community service. Requiring a priest whose calling includes serving the homeless to perform community service might also be seen as one of our nation's most astute sentences.

These twin interests and episodes (caring for the poor and protesting militarism) offer a window not only on Baxter's vision of Christian commitment in the public sphere but also on his integration of faith and learn-

ing in the university. Baxter's scholarship has largely focused on responding to the "Americanist" tradition in Catholic social and political thought
through the resources of the Catholic Worker and Catholic Peace movements. Baxter calls this the Catholic "Radicalist" tradition and juxtaposes
it against the Catholic "Americanist" tradition. This Americanist tradition was exemplified by the Jesuit scholar John Courtney Murray (and
numerous others) who affirmed that the guiding principles of American
polity fit neatly with Catholic doctrine and social teachings.

According to Baxter, the difference between the Radicalist and the
Americanist traditions "turns on different understandings of the nature of
the *polis* in social ethics. Briefly put, in the Americanist tradition, the
*polis* is identified with the modern state, in particular the United States of
America, and as a result, the state is seen as the primary mechanism for
the implementation of justice." Baxter notes that in the Radicalist tradition, "the *polis* is identified with Christ and the church, and with smaller,
practice-based communities whose forms of life are closely patterned after
the body of Christ and the church."[4]

It is not Baxter's intent to discredit Murray (whom he describes as "one of
the greatest Catholic theologians this country has ever had").[5] Baxter affirms that Murray should be credited for helping to move Catholics, in the
1950s and 1960s, away from the notion that "the normative church-state
arrangement was the 'confessional state'—in which Catholicism is the established religion of the state." But Baxter is critical of Murray "because he
simply assumed that the Church should find a congenial home in the United
States of America. He didn't see clearly enough how Catholic political theory and Catholic social teaching would run into conflict with the political
assumptions of the modern liberal democratic state." Baxter continues:

> Murray himself was critical of secularism. But I maintain that he failed to
> provide us with the resources to resist it. He believed that Catholics should
> join with others to develop a "public discourse" based on reason alone. And

---

[4]Michael J. Baxter, "Notes on Catholic Americanism and Catholic Radicalism: Toward a Counter-
Tradition of Catholic Social Ethics," in *American Catholic Traditions: Resources for Renewal*, ed.
Sandra Yocum Mize and William L. Portier (Maryknoll, N.Y.: Orbis, 1997), p. 53.
[5]Michael Baxter, quoted in William Bole, "Is America All Too Much with Us?" *Our Sunday Visitor*
85, no. 52 (1997): 11.

so this discourse is virtually devoid of any meaningful reference to Christ, the Scriptures, the liturgy, the lives of the saints. . . .

But as I see it, this strategy has back-fired. Instead of bolstering the secular discourse of the nation, it has secularized the political discourse of the Church. At any rate, Murray believed that the Church should dedicate itself to the project of developing a public ethic for the nation.[6]

This Americanist tradition has bred a mentality which, both by design and default, has proposed that in this moment of cultural crisis Catholicism has the resources to save America. Baxter calls this the "American Catholics to the rescue" mentality. He believes it was present in the post-World War I period; it was present in the 1950s and after in Murray; and it is present today in the form of neoconservative cultural warriors like Richard John Neuhaus and George Weigel, senior fellow at the Ethics and Public Policy Center. This effort, in and of itself, would not be so bad (though he finds it hopelessly naive) except that those who would save America end up subordinated to America. And those "who declare their allegiance to the democratic state . . . end up legitimating the violence necessary to protect it." For Baxter, this issue boils down to dual political disjunctions: in which *polis* (the nation-state or practiced-based communities) will one find the resources for the implementation of justice and in which *polis* will one find a faith worth dying for?

## RESPONSE TO THE BAXTER CONTROVERSY

The *Chronicle of Higher Education* described the controversy surrounding Baxter's visiting appointment in its "Faculty Notes" section of the December 13, 1996, issue. The *Chronicle* asserted (erroneously) that Baxter's appointment had come against the unanimous recommendation of the department. The event was also the subject of an article in the *National Catholic Reporter*. Pamela Schaeffer described how the priest had been "imposed on the faculty," and "[f]ollowing months of controversy, the university's Faculty Senate denounced the president's administrative style in a formal resolution."[7] Schaeffer did note that it was the five-member

---

[6]Ibid.
[7]Pamela Schaeffer, "Irish Fighting: Faculty Denounces ND President," *National Catholic Reporter*, December 13, 1996.

theology appointments committee and not the entire theology department that had unanimously opposed Baxter's hiring.

Baxter was not, however, without his supporters. Fifteen scholars from
six prestigious universities who knew Baxter and his scholarship responded
with a letter to the *Chronicle of Higher Education* correcting its assertion
that departmental opposition to Baxter's appointment was unanimous and
affirming that they were "highly impressed" with his scholarly work. The
fifteen signatories were Scott Appleby, John Garvey, Philip Gleason,
George Marsden, Marvin O'Connell and David Solomon from Notre
Dame; Frank Lentricchia, Kenneth Surin, Alasdair MacIntyre (then)
from Duke; Robert George, Leigh Schmidt and Robert Wuthnow from
Princeton; Thomas Hibbs (then) from Boston College; Beth Wenger from
Pennsylvania; and Ruth Marie Griffith from Northwestern.[8]

Other Notre Dame colleagues David Burrell, CSC, (Hesburgh Professor of Philosophy and Theology) and Alfred Freddoso (Professor of Philosophy) both wrote responses to the *National Catholic Reporter*. In Burrell's letter of December 11, 1996, he expressed mystery over the entire
incident. Why should such an extraordinarily well-qualified candidate be
rejected? Not because of any bias against CSC priests since "discrimina-
tion against the Congregation of Holy Cross would hardly characterize
the Department of Theology." Burrell believed the answer lay in the fact
that "many extraneous factors impeded a clear appreciation of [Baxter's]
intellectual prowess as well as of his potential to carry forward theological
discussion with those willing to engage in a thoroughgoing inquiry."[9]

What are the extraneous factors? Apparently one of the dominant factors was the issue of Baxter's dissertation director, Stanley Hauerwas, to
which Malloy alluded. Indeed, Burrell also notes that this connection was
problematic for Baxter. Freddoso noted "an ongoing and nasty feud between [Baxter's] dissertation director, a former Notre Dame theologian,
and several senior members of the theology department." Richard P.

---

[8]Only three signatures (Solomon, Lentricchia and Wuthnow) appeared in the *Chronicle* (February
7, 1997) because of its policy of printing no more than three for any given letter. All of the signatures appeared in the *Notre Dame Observer*, February 6, 1997.
[9]David Burrell to the *National Catholic Reporter*, excerpted by Pamela Schaeffer, "Notre Dame Dispute May Signal a Shift: Countercultural Catholic Voice Stirs a Storm," *National Catholic Reporter*,
January 31, 1997.

McBrien (Crowley-O'Brien-Walter Professor of Theology) denied that such was the case. Malloy, Burrell, Freddoso and many others on campus thought otherwise. Their sentiments seemed confirmed in department chair Cunningham's assessment of Baxter's dissertation. Cunningham wrote, "He [Baxter] also shows traces of his mentor's habits of pugnaciousness and bombast but in conversation pulls back when challenged."[10]

Feuds, rumors of feuds and rampant pugnaciousness are neither new nor uncommon to the academy. On the contrary, the old joke about why academic politics is so dirty (because the stakes are so small) seems confirmed on every campus in the country, from the most obscure community college to the most visible research university. Thus, in many respects, the Baxter situation was unremarkable, however much grief, pain and mistrust it may have bred in South Bend. My interest in this event lies in why the appointment of a clearly radical priest, supported by Daniel Berrigan and lauded in the pages of newspapers like the *Houston Catholic Worker*,[11] generated animosity at such a bulwark of the Catholic and religious left as the Notre Dame theology department. And to understand this we have to turn to Pamela Schaeffer's second *National Catholic Reporter* article.[12]

The *National Catholic Reporter* describes itself as "The Independent, Lay-edited Catholic Newsweekly." It is a veritable mainstay of the liberal Catholic establishment in the United States. Its pages regularly report the institutional silencing of dissident priests and the progress of liberationist and base community movements in Latin America and elsewhere; its editorials frequently call for the Catholic Church to embrace more "democratic" procedures for the establishment of accepted doctrine and practice. The *National Catholic Reporter* has long valued the unique contributions of leftist Catholic scholars, priests and activists; indeed, Richard McBrien has at times had a regular column appear in its pages. It is for this reason that the *National Catholic Reporter*'s positive assessment of Baxter is so interesting and so important.

---

[10]Lawrence Cunningham, cited in Robert G. Blakey, "Dissenting Views," p. 10. Notre Dame Faculty Senate Academic Affairs Committee Report, November 7, 1996.

[11]"Student Finds God at Notre Dame," "Is Dorothy Day's Laetare Medal in Jeopardy?" and "ND Professor defends Baxter," *Houston Catholic Worker* 17, no. 1 (1997).

[12]Schaeffer, "Notre Dame Dispute May Signal a Shift," pp. 3-6.

In this second article, Schaeffer recognized that the controversy at Notre Dame focused on a "question critical to American Catholicism—the right relationship of Catholicism to culture, of religion to politics." Though on the surface the question appeared to be why a bright and accomplished priest failed to gain the support of the department, "under the surface lurks a youthful challenge to American Catholicism's old guard." Baxter represented a shift, according to Schaeffer, "in the way Catholicism is defined and practiced in the United States. Baxter's allies say he blows apart the usual liberal-conservative categories that have often been used to describe Catholics since the Second Vatican Council in the 1960s."[13]

During the spring and summer of 1997, as the controversy surrounding Baxter's appointment moved even further onto the national Catholic stage, the prescience of Schaeffer's observation ("a youthful challenge" which "blows apart the usual liberal-conservative categories") became ever more apparent. In April 1997, *Our Sunday Visitor*, one of the nation's most popular and most widely read weekly Catholic newspapers, ran a three-week series on Baxter and the question of whether "Catholics in this country [are] saving the culture or being enslaved by it."[14] The series consisted of a lengthy interview with Baxter the first week, a response to Baxter's critique of "Americanism" by nine Catholic intellectuals in the second week and Baxter's response to their comments in the third week. As was his practice throughout the controversy, Baxter refused to talk about his appointment at Notre Dame but only about his larger critique of Americanism. (It is, perhaps, worth noting that he also assumed this posture with me in our conversations, and this reticence initially made it difficult to get "Baxter's side" of the story about the furor over his appointment.)

But others have "taken up Baxter's side"—despite his protestations—and some of these supporters have come from some unlikely sources. As noted previously, the bilingual *Houston Catholic Worker* newspaper, edited by Mark Zwick and Louise Zwick, ran its first article on the Baxter affair in its January-February 1997 issue. That issue contained two articles that responded to the Notre Dame situation and a reprint of Alfred Freddoso's

---

[13]Ibid., p. 3.
[14]Bole, "Is America All Too Much with Us?" p. 9.

letter to the *National Catholic Reporter.* In its March-April issue the Zwicks continued to address the issue, answering the question, "Why argue about Father Baxter and Notre Dame?" The Zwicks answered that, in Schaeffer's second *National Catholic Reporter* article, Father McBrien (of the Notre Dame theology department) was on the record as having labeled the Catholic Worker and the Catholic Peace movements as "sects." The Zwicks saw this action (and the rejection of Baxter) as attempts "to marginalize them from the Catholic tradition."[15] On the contrary, the Zwicks argued that it is in reality the Americanist tradition which

> might more properly be called "sectarian" because they [the Americanists] respond to the tensions between Church and world by restricting religion to a private affair and going along with everyone else in the public arena. This has never been the Catholic tradition.[16]

(The questions "Who—and what—are the sectarians?" and "Why should we care?" are more complicated than they appear. I will address these matters in chapter four.)

The Zwicks point out that the liberal Catholicism of Father McBrien turns out to be another "strange bedfellow" with the neoconservatism of Catholic thinkers like Weigel. Both thinkers affirm the fundamental compatibility of the dominant American ways of life and thought with traditional Catholic thought—even though they frequently construe these ways of life and thought very differently. This was also the argument made by David Schindler (editor of the English language edition of the journal *Communio* and professor at the John Paul II Institute for Studies on Marriage and Family in Washington, D.C.) in *Heart of the World, Center of the Church.*[17] Schindler is one who "applauds and amplifies Baxter's critique of liberal democracy and the consumer society" in the *Our Sunday Visitor* series.[18]

The "strange bedfellow" argument was also made by John Schmalz-

[15]Mark Zwick and Louise Zwick, "Why Argue About Fr. Baxter and Notre Dame?" *Houston Catholic Worker* 17, no. 2 (March-April 1997): 1.

[16]Ibid., p. 6.

[17]David L. Schindler, *Heart of the World, Center of the Church: Communio Ecclesiology, Liberalism, and Liberation* (Grand Rapids: Eerdmans, 1996).

[18]Bole, "Is America All Too Much with Us?" p. 12.

bauer in an article in the spring 1997 issue of *re:generation Quarterly*, an unfortunately short-lived glossy and stylish magazine for orthodox Generation Xers. Schmalzbauer's essay, playing on the recent conservative ecumenism, was titled "(Conservative) Evangelicals and (Liberal) Catholics Together." Despite the fact that, in terms of format and presentation, *re:generation Quarterly* could hardly have been any more different from the *Houston Catholic Worker*, the argument and appraisal of the Baxter situation turned out to be quite similar. Schmalzbauer pointed out the similarities between the Religious Right's and Liberal American Catholicism's propagation of the "myth of the marriage of the Christian faith and American values." Schmalzbauer continued,

> In a strange paradox, both the evangelical partisans of the religious right and the liberal Catholic advocates of the Americanized church have romanticized the relation between the Christian faith and the American nation. Neoconservative Catholics have been little better in this regard, emphasizing a basic harmony between America's political creed and a Christian public philosophy.[19]

Schmalzbauer used the Baxter situation at Notre Dame to make a further point about "the mission of Christian higher education in the decades to come." In his view, "both Catholics and evangelicals will have to choose between a watered-down hybrid of Christian faith and civil religion and a more radical proclamation of the Gospel story."[20]

The mission of Christian higher education, the integration of faith and learning in the public space of higher education, really is the issue here, and the question boils down to what extent should faith be allowed to participate in the politics which is the ordered life of the *polis?* The Notre Dame theology department represented, in the words of Richard John Neuhaus, a "flabby and uncritical accommodationism" characterized by a "readiness to trim Catholic distinctives in order not to offend cultural sensibilities."[21]

---

[19]John Schmalzbauer, "(Conservative) Evangelicals and (Liberal) Catholics Together," *re:generation Quarterly* 3, no. 2 (1997): 33-34.

[20]Ibid., p. 35.

[21]Richard John Neuhaus, "Michael Baxter and the Theological Salad Bar," *First Things* 73 (1997): 62.

This "delicate" description comes in Neuhaus's own assessment of the controversy over Baxter's appointment. Neuhaus first weighed in on the Baxter affair in the April and May 1997 editions of *First Things*. In "Michael Baxter and the Theological Salad Bar," Neuhaus, who has no great love for Notre Dame, briefly described the controversy, proclaiming, "Amidst all the charges and countercharges, I confess to finding myself in an unusual position"; that is, Neuhaus is not quite sure what to do with Baxter. Neuhaus believes that "Baxter is on most questions a theological conservative, but on matters social and political he is pretty much an unexpurgated lefty."[22] (On the surface that position is not so different from Neuhaus's own "quadrilateral" mentioned earlier.) And despite the fact that Neuhaus thinks that Baxter (and Hauerwas) "are wrong about many things, but they are intelligently wrong on things very much worth arguing about," Neuhaus believes that Baxter's contributions "are very much needed by the bland and wilting salad bar Catholicism of the Notre Dame theology department."[23] (The salad bar analogy comes from former chair of the theology department Lawrence Cunningham. Cunningham had made the comment that "the Catholic tradition is like a big salad bar. . . . There are a lot of different things you can put on your plate, and one of those is a religious identity that stands against the predominant culture." According to Neuhaus, "It's hard to have a really good argument with a salad bar.")

Neuhaus does not know what to do with Baxter because (like Baxter) he believes that "authentic Christianity must be, in many respects, emphatically countercultural." But (unlike Baxter) he wants to support, albeit critically, certain "aspects of the American condition" that Baxter wants "to unambiguously assault."

Baxter's three-year visiting appointment at Notre Dame came to an end at the close of the spring 1999 academic year. During those three years Baxter continued to write, publish and speak on a variety of topics. And though his appointment and presence remained controversial to some faculty, his passionate ministry and inspiring teaching made him a favor-

---

[22]Neuhaus, "Michael Baxter," pp. 61-62.
[23]Ibid., p. 62.

ite of many students[24] and helped him overcome his rocky start to become a valued colleague among many faculty. In April 1999, Baxter was invited to accept a full-time tenure track appointment as assistant professor of theology at Notre Dame. Subsequently, however, Baxter voluntarily took a nontenure-track position of "associate professional specialist in theology." This allowed him to devote more of his time to the (Catholic Worker) Peter Claver House and Our Lady of the Road daytime drop-in center in South Bend, while continuing his scholarly work on the history of Catholic Radicalism in twentieth-century America. In 2006, Baxter sought laicization and release from his priestly vocation. This request was granted in 2007.

Clearly, Baxter, like Neuhaus, defies easy characterization. Standardbearers on both the Right and the Left do not know what to do with him. In this case, however, Neuhaus himself has become a rather difficult fellow to figure out and clearly is not a standard-bearer for the Right. My observation is that Baxter renders traditional sensibilities about religion and the Left problematic in much the same way that the *First Things* symposium creates difficulties for how one is to understand religion and the Right. But how do these two events illumine reflection on the limits of Liberal democracy? It is to this question that we now turn.

---

[24]Colleen Carroll, *The New Faithful: Why Young Adults Are Embracing Christian Orthodoxy* (Chicago: Loyola Press, 2004), p. 204.

# 4

# RIVAL VERSIONS
# OF CONFESSIONALISM

## Neuhaus and Baxter

SOME MIGHT QUESTION BOTH THE SIGNIFICANCE of and the connection between these events. The Baxter affair might be just another squabble between university administrators and faculty, not unlike the sorts of disputes that erupt every year on every campus in the land. Furthermore, could the *First Things* symposium possibly be more than just a tempest in a teapot? Francis Fukuyama was correct: it is hard to imagine "Richard John Neuhaus holed up in a farmhouse shooting it out with ATF officers anytime soon."[1] Viewed from the perspective of a decade later, one might conclude that the composition of a George W. Bush–appointed Roberts Court surely changes how conservatives feel about judicial activism. Moreover, isn't the Baxter situation rendered moot by his choosing to devote more of his time to those struggling on the streets of inner-city South Bend than to those studying under the campus's famous golden dome?

[1]Francis Fukuyama, "On the Future of Conservatism," *Commentary*, February 1997, p. 27.

The significance of these events lies not in their "resolution" (what has happened since 1997) but in how these events highlight the inadequacy of most of our contemporary understandings of the proper nature, purpose and relation of politics and faith. In the case of these two events, they are connected in some interesting and provocative ways, and viewing them together enables us to make sense of the larger conversation on Christian faith and Liberal democracy. As stated at the end of chapter three, it is my contention that just as Neuhaus and the *First Things* symposium have wreaked havoc with traditional sensibilities about religion and politics on the Right, so Baxter's situation has rendered problematic the traditional sensibilities about religion and politics on the Left. Viewed together, these events offer a window through which to view the incoherence of Enlightenment Liberalism's status quo and present us with an opportunity to think again about the inherently political nature of Christian faith.

In this chapter I address why these two events ought to be viewed together and why they are significant for evangelicals, mainline Protestants and secularists. I argue that the ambiguity surrounding the principals is mirrored in their different understandings of the relation of confessional faith to natural law. Here we see operating rival versions of the relationship that natural law plays between politics and faith. For lack of a better term, Christian postmodernists (like Hauerwas and Baxter) are tempted to redescribe politics in favor of a Christian particularism. Christian modernists (like Neuhaus) who have previously been tempted to use natural law to support Enlightenment Liberalism (understood as neoconservative politics and economics) now find themselves at a moment of crisis concerning how to speak about natural law without abandoning their more foundational Christian confessional commitments or alienating their secular political compatriots. A third alternative can be seen in secular Liberals (like Gertrude Himmelfarb) who long for the good old days in which a chastened view of natural law amounted to little more than an appeal to religiously neutral morality. The crucial recent development, as I see it, is the growing recognition by certain Christian thinkers (such as Wes Avram, Michael Budde, Robert Brimlow, Craig A. Carter, William Cavanaugh, Barry Harvey, Ralph Wood and John Wright—to name only a few)[2] that there can be no easy rapprochement between Christianity and Enlightenment Liberalism. Before turning to these questions, however, it is important to see the close relation between these events.

## HOW ARE THESE EVENTS CONNECTED?

There are a number of individuals whose projects and associations are intertwined with both the Michael Baxter and *First Things* controversies. Some of these individuals have been major contributors toward the emerging critique of Enlightenment Liberalism. Alasdair MacIntyre, who signed the national letter of support for Baxter, certainly stands at the top of any such list. Through his volumes *After Virtue, Whose Justice? Which Rationality?* and *Three Rival Versions of Moral Enquiry*, he has done as much as anyone else to call into question the hegemony of Enlightenment Liberalism. George Marsden and Robert Wuthnow have played similar roles (though both have affirmed aspects of Liberalism even in their critiques): Marsden with respect to history and the role of religion in higher education and Wuthnow with respect to the sociology of the American religious experience. As noted earlier, Robert George, one of the original *First Things* symposiasts, was also one of the fifteen signatories to the letter of support for Baxter which appeared in the *Chronicle of Higher Education* and the *Notre Dame Observer*.

The most obvious individual relevant to both events is, of course, Stanley Hauerwas, Baxter's dissertation director and (at the time of the 1996 symposium) a member of the *First Things* editorial board (from which Himmelfarb and Berger resigned). Described by *Lingua Franca*'s David Glenn as "impossible-to-pigeonhole," Hauerwas expressed support for the *First Things* symposium: "I think it shows that the magazine has great integrity." Hauerwas continues, "The problem isn't with the courts. The

---

[2]Wes Avram, ed., *Anxious About Empire: Theological Essays on the New Global Realities* (Grand Rapids: Brazos, 2004); Michael Budde and John Wright, eds., *Coflicting Allegiances: The Church-Based University in a Liberal Democratic Society* (Grand Rapids: Brazos, 2004); Michael Budde and Robert Brimlow, eds., *The Church as Counterculture* (Albany: SUNY, 2004); Craig A. Carter, *Rethinking Christ and Culture: A Post-Christendom Perspective* (Grand Rapids: Brazos, 2006); William T. Cavanaugh, *Theopolitical Imagination* (London: T & T Clark, 2002); Barry Harvey, *Another City: An Ecclesiological Primer for a Post-Christian World* (Harrisburg, Penn.: Trinity Press International, 1999); Ralph Wood, *Contending for the Faith: The Church's Engagement with Culture* (Waco, Tex.: Baylor University Press, 2003).

problem is the American people! The conservatives don't want to admit that this is what the American people want! They want assisted suicide! They believe in autonomy!"[3] These allegedly "autonomous Americans" are the embodiment of Enlightenment Liberalism.

One of the most obvious similarities between Baxter and the *First Things* symposiasts is also one of the most odd. Both were labeled "anti-American." To be specific, Heilbrunn accused the *First Things* editors' Thomism of being "not so much anti-American as un-American," and David Brooks's entire essay in the *Weekly Standard* was titled "The Right's Anti-American Temptation."[4] These are curious charges to be leveled against "conservatives"—especially conservatives like Neuhaus who are frequently accused of being the brains of the "God and country" Religious Right.

As for Baxter, since he has consistently articulated a critique of the "Americanist" impulse in Catholic thought, the charge of "anti-Americanism" might come as no surprise. What is curious, however, is from where the charge came. Then chairman of the Notre Dame theology department Lawrence Cunningham had written in his analysis of Baxter's dissertation, "The supreme irony, of course, is that Baxter wants an appointment in an institution that is the embodiment of the Americanist tradition. How does Baxter hope to be a member of a community which holds up as its ideal: God, Country, and Notre Dame?"[5] In his letter to the *National Catholic Reporter*, Alfred Freddoso of the Notre Dame philosophy department responded, "As far as I know, other departments in the University do not use nationalism as a criterion for appointment."[6] Cunningham later reported to Pamela Schaeffer that his comment (though included in his official evaluation of Baxter's dissertation) was made in jest.

The irony of Cunningham's accusation (jest or no) extends far beyond Freddoso's jab. Academic departments at major American universities are one of the last places one would expect to find inordinate nationalism.

---

[3]Stanley Hauerwas, cited in David Glenn, "The Schism," *Lingua Franca*, February 1997, p. 26.
[4]Jacob Heilbrunn, "Neocon v. Theocon," *New Republic*, December 30, 1996, p. 24; David Brooks, "The Right's Anti-American Temptation," *Weekly Standard*, November 11, 1996, pp. 23-26.
[5]Lawrence Cunningham, cited in Pamela Schaeffer, "Notre Dame Dispute May Signal a Shift: Countercultural Catholic Voice Stirs a Storm," *National Catholic Reporter*, January 31, 1997.
[6]Alfred Freddoso, cited in Schaeffer, "Notre Dame Dispute May Signal a Shift."

Surely the Notre Dame theology department is not so different in this regard. One would have thought that Baxter's critique would be appealing to a traditionally liberal department of theology like Notre Dame's, but such was not the case. Moreover, the presence of an alternative vision like Baxter's seems compatible with the current academic preoccupation with multiculturalism, diversity and pluralism. But again, such turned out to be not the case. How then are we to understand the commitment to Americanism?

When Schaeffer asked Richard McBrien if the unpopular nature of Baxter's views about the Americanist tradition was the reason for his rejection, McBrien replied, "I'm saying [the countercultural approach] is not representative of the Catholic tradition. It's like a dissenting opinion. Should it be represented? Of course. Should it be over represented? I hope not." Schaeffer noted that McBrien believed that Baxter's view was at the time adequately represented in the theology department by John Howard Yoder, a Mennonite.[7] (Yoder died December 30, 1997.) Of course, Baxter is not a Mennonite, and whatever similar commitments Baxter and Yoder may have shared about counterculturalism, Baxter represents a challenge to Catholic coherence and faithfulness that Yoder did not. And this, of course, is the heart of the matter.

Baxter's work poses a challenge to this "Catholics to the rescue" mentality which is embodied in the Americanist tradition. It is obvious that an Americanist Catholic who might be intrigued by Yoder might reject Baxter, precisely because Yoder's work does not pose an internal challenge to Catholic sensibilities in the way that Baxter does. Neither Schaeffer nor McBrien commented on whether there was another Catholic theologian at Notre Dame who affirmed Baxter's position.

McBrien's position, then, in the end seems only committed to superficial or cosmetic diversity. One should not fault McBrien here; his position is the unfortunate (and, incidentally, conceptually incoherent) position of most of the larger national academic culture. Stanley Fish has described this commitment to "superficial or cosmetic" diversity as a "boutique multiculturalism" that inevitably arises within the Liberal attempt to make

---

[7]Schaeffer, "Notre Dame Dispute May Signal a Shift."

sense of difference. According to Fish, "Boutique multiculturalists will always stop short of approving other cultures at a point where some value at
their center generates an act that offends against the canons of civilized
decency."[8] In the end the differing vision cannot be tolerated because it
calls into question the core commitments of the establishment vision. Baxter (and Neuhaus—but for different reasons) represents just such a deep
challenge to the core commitments of an establishment vision that has
consistently sought to wed Christian and Catholic social teaching and doctrine to the public polity of Enlightenment Liberalism, American-style.

The superficial similarity between these prominent Catholics is that
they have both found themselves (or taken up stances) at odds with the
Notre Dame theology department, the bastion of just that establishment
vision. But that in itself is not particularly significant given Baxter's and
Neuhaus's differences in both belief and circumstances. The more significant similarity is the explicit opposition this confrontation represents for
theologically motivated countercultural politics. And this leads us to the
most important similarity to be found in these two events and in these
two principal actors.

This willingness to call into question the core Liberal commitments of
the Enlightenment establishment vision becomes the overriding connection between both Richard John Neuhaus and Michael Baxter. Both have
demonstrated a willingness to go against the grain by proposing theologically countercultural alternatives. In a world where all politics is reduced
to statecraft, the only theologically countercultural alternatives most Liberals (either religious or nonreligious) can imagine is a theocracy or confessional state or some kind of retreat from political life altogether. Neither Baxter nor Neuhaus advocate a theocratic or confessional political
order—though Neuhaus was routinely accused of such before, during and
after the *First Things* upheaval. Both do offer varied normative analyses,
and both appeal to natural law to make their cases, but they construe
natural law in different ways.

The arguments against theologically countercultural alternatives typically run in the following way. Politics understood as statecraft means that

---

[8]Stanley Fish, "Boutique Multiculturalism, or Why Liberals are Incapable of Thinking About Hate
Speech," *Critical Inquiry* 23 (Winter 1997): 378.

political action will be one of either engagement or political retreat. Consider first the question of political engagement. If one proposes to be theologically countercultural, then democratic Liberalism and theocracy (or the confessional state) are viewed as the only options. Failure to endorse Liberalism entails that one must affirm theocracy; hesitancy to endorse theocracy means that one is really a Liberal undercover. It is read as a simple disjunctive syllogism. W. Robert Aufill of Stillwater, Oklahoma, made just this argument. Responding to Neuhaus's commentary on Baxter, Mr. Aufill recalls a personal exchange with Baxter in which he "hesitated" to defend the confessional state. Aufill sees this as evidence of Baxter's abiding Liberalism. Baxter responded by noting,

> I still hesitate. I distrust attempts to provide an account of "the state" in the abstract because such attempts legitimate what is in the name of what ought to be. I especially distrust such accounts in modernity because, as Alasdair MacIntyre has argued, the modern nation-state is a dangerous and unmanageable institution that often masquerades as an embodiment of community and a repository of sacred values. Faced with this situation, the Church does not need a theory of the state. What the Church needs is a description of the true character of the state and a set of practices to resist it. To designate the modern nation-state as an instrument by which to propagate the Christian faith is to imperil the Christian faith.[9]

This statement certainly warrants further discussion, and it is one to which I will return.

Neuhaus for his part has sharply criticized the theocratic "alternatives" as well. Neuhaus has described the Christian reconstructionist (theocratic) movement as a "moralizing and legalizing of the Gospel of God's grace [which] is a dull heresy peddled to disappointed people who are angry because they have not received what they had no good reason to expect."[10]

Not only has Neuhaus criticized the reconstructionist movement, he has also consistently rejected the proposition that the United States is a "Christian nation" in any sense other than a blandly demographic one

---

[9]Michael Baxter, "Correspondence," *First Things* 75 (August-September 1997): 6.
[10]Richard John Neuhaus, "Why Wait for the Kingdom? The Theonomist Temptation" *First Things* 3 (May 1990): 21.

with respect to how most Americans describe themselves. The widely recognized 1997 ecumenical statement "We Hold These Truths" is explicit in its denial of the "Christian nation" hypothesis. That statement (which Neuhaus not only signed but also had no small part in producing) asserts: "We reject the idea that ours should be a 'Christian nation.' We do not seek a sacred public square but a civil public square."[11]

If both Baxter and Neuhaus reject the alleged dilemma of necessarily affirming either Liberalism or theocracy, then, one must reasonably ask, what do they propose in the way of theologically countercultural alternatives? My answer to this question lies at the heart of this book. Before getting to their answers, however, it seems to me that the first and most important point to recognize is that they (and others, as we shall see) are seeking to articulate these alternatives and that they have begun to get a hearing. The uproar caused by the systematic misreading and misinterpretation of their ideas is precisely what leads us to recognize that alternative paradigms are in play. The answer to the question lies in the cultivation of various models of extraordinary politics that are not merely reducible to statecraft. In the closing chapters of the volume I will attempt to articulate what this extraordinary politics looks like and point to some options (beyond Baxter and Neuhaus) that are currently available.

Neuhaus and Baxter have remarkably differing visions. Both appeal to natural law to substantiate their claims. Natural law, however, comes out looking quite different in their rival propositions. Neuhaus believes that the natural law can be known apart from religious traditions and is the basis for all positive law. On this question of the church's politics, Neuhaus usually seems content to call the citizens of the United States (many of whom are members of the Christian church) back to what he sees as a genuine representative democracy. On this understanding, legitimate government is based on the consent of the governed, and the public law (made and enforced by the various branches of this government) neither grievously contradicts the natural law nor requires its citizens to perform or abstain from performing actions the morality of which is dictated by that natural law. Until recently, Neuhaus was more optimistic (he would per-

---

[11]"We Hold These Truths," *First Things* 76 (October 1997): 53.

haps say "guardedly optimistic") that such an arrangement could be worked out. In the year following the original *First Things* symposium, Neuhaus repeatedly argued that there are in principle no reasons why such an arrangement cannot be achieved; any recent hesitancy is based merely on the practical (i.e., praxalogical) difficulties for democracy that arise when the validity of natural law is denied by many who are charged with creating, interpreting and enforcing public law. The Catholic and religious commitment and optimism to working out just such an arrangement (despite the difficulties) is the abiding legacy of John Courtney Murray.

Beginning in the October 1999 issue of *First Things*, Father Neuhaus published a three-part offering under the title "Proposing Democracy Anew." Neuhaus appealed to his oft-repeated quip that the phrase "Christian America" is "a description under the judgment of an aspiration."[12] Over the next three issues he offered ten proposals about what makes democracy "both possible and necessary." According to Neuhaus, "The proposals are closely connected to Judeo–Christian presuppositions and, more specifically, to Catholic social teaching." To understand Neuhaus's perspective, one must understand the significance of the following maxim: (A) *Politics is in largest part the function of culture, and at the heart of culture is morality, and at the heart of morality is religion.*[13] Neuhaus has repeated this claim, in public presentations and in print, on several occasions.

This maxim initially presents itself as persuasive, but upon closer examination it has several difficulties. My suspicion arises from a series of problems, rendering the syllogism-like maxim both logically dubious and, in turn, unsound. First, it is not really a syllogism. Notions like "in largest part the function" and "at the heart of" are vague and nonspecific. They are neither identity statements nor statements of function. They identify some inductive relationships, rendered metaphorically, that suggest further relationships, but they do not show any determinate properties or relations. Second, there is the problem of equivocation. As Neuhaus articulates this statement, there is an equivocation with either the term *mo-*

---

[12]Richard John Neuhaus, "Proposing Democracy Anew—Part One," *First Things* 96 (October 1999): 87.

[13]Richard John Neuhaus, "Proposing Democracy Anew—Part Two," *First Things* 97 (November 1999): 90.

*rality* or the term *religion* (or both). The "morality" at the heart of politically informed culture is morality broadly construed; it is precisely that morality of culture which is necessary for the sustenance of a viable democratic polity. It is no mean feat; it is the morality of truth-telling, of courageous acts, of taking responsibility for one's actions, of generous giving and gracious receiving. It is not uniquely or particularly Christian. It is exhibited daily by Christians and non-Christians alike. It is also, sadly, forgotten and ignored on a daily basis by Christians and non-Christians alike. At the heart of this morality is civil religion.

The morality at the heart of *confessional* religion is a very particular religious morality. It is, in the words of Søren Kierkegaard's pseudonym Johannes de Silentio, an absolute duty to obey God.[14] It recognizes the hierarchy of sovereignties (which Neuhaus also recognizes), and it cultivates those virtues that make for the proper flourishing of the one who would worship in spirit and in truth. It is dangerous and prone to self-deception. It is the object of derision and scorn by the cultured despisers, and is blamed (sometimes rightly) for everything from illiteracy and kitsch art to terrorism and war. Nevertheless, the difference between morality broadly construed and confessional, religious morality cannot be underestimated. This is the difference between Kierkegaard's ethical and religious spheres, between the knight of infinite resignation and the knight of faith.

Put this way, it seems that there are now two possible revised versions of the Neuhaus maxim: (B) *Politics is in largest part the function of the common culture, and at the heart of the common culture is a broadly construed morality. At the heart of this broadly construed morality is civil religion.* Or (C) *Politics is in largest part the function of the common culture, and at the heart of the common culture is a religious morality. At the heart of this religious morality is confessional religion.*

(B) is probably true, but it is in no way a satisfactory account of religion for Christians, and Neuhaus is surely no proponent of such an arrangement. (C) is false, though for many decades it might have appeared to be true given the veneer of an ostensibly "Christian" society or nation. There

---

[14]Søren Kierkegaard, *Fear and Trembling*, trans. Howard V. Hong and Edna H. Hong (Princeton, N.J.: Princeton University Press, 1983), p. 68.

are, of course, many in our society who believe (C), or in the case of anti-religious detractors, want to use belief in (C) to scare those who are nervous about "fundamentalism" (equivocations here notwithstanding). In our post-Constantinian period, it seems to me, even the plausibility of (C) diminishes with every passing day. The common culture is one of convenience and consumption; the widespread acceptable inability to distinguish, and the disinterest in distinguishing, the legal from the ethical in the Enron and related accounting scandals is evidence of just how broad such broadly construed morality can become.

Baxter can agree with neither Neuhaus's description nor his aspirations for Christian America. For him, America can only be described as a Christian nation in the most banal, sentimental and superficial ways. Baxter wants to focus the church's "politics" on the cultivation of small communities which have their life in the liturgy and the sacraments of the church and which, in turn, make human flourishing possible. Such a flourishing has its basis in the natural law, but the natural law can only be fully known with respect to its supernatural life in Christ and the church. Baxter (as well as other critics like David Schindler and William Portier) criticizes Neuhaus and the "theocons" for assuming that an easy peace can be reached between the Catholic tradition (the demands of the church) and the secular polity of the United States (the demands of the nation-state). Baxter sees this commitment as exemplified most clearly in the political thought of John Courtney Murray and updated in the work of Neuhaus.

On this latter point Neuhaus has noted, "I do not believe the Catholic tradition 'unequivocally endorses' the political order of the U.S. I emphatically reject such a view."[15] Both men then are committed to the proposition that the "politics" that orders our lives together is to be fundamentally a theologically informed politics which does not degenerate into either a secular Liberalism or a theocracy. That Neuhaus's and Baxter's analyses and appeals to natural law turn out to be quite different is not the primary point at this juncture. The primary point is that both Neuhaus (guardedly) and Baxter (emphatically) reject the notion that it is always

---

[15]Richard John Neuhaus, "Correspondence," *First Things* 75 (August-September 1997): 5.

possible to be both faithful Christians and "good Americans." In the introduction to the original *First Things* symposium, Neuhaus wrote:

> "God and country" is a motto that has in the past come easily, some would
> say too easily, to almost all Americans. What are the cultural and political
> consequences when many more Americans, perhaps even a majority, come
> to the conclusion that the question is "God *or* country"?[16]

What are the consequences indeed?

## RESIDENT ALIENS AND RELUCTANT SECTARIANS

Charles Colson referred to Stanley Hauerwas in his contribution to the original *First Things* symposium. Colson seemed to agree with David Smolin's conclusion that in an increasingly hostile environment religious believers will be forced either "to abandon their religious beliefs and accommodate themselves to an amoral, libertarian regime" or abandon "their political interests, becoming what the theologian Stanley Hauerwas has called 'resident aliens' in America—no longer concerned about the fortunes or misfortunes of a flawed republic, no longer considering this land their country."[17] (David Brooks cited this passage as evidence of the "anti-American" temptation in his piece in the *Weekly Standard*.)

Colson's presentation here of Hauerwas's position is misleading and takes the second horn of the dilemma ("political retreat") described earlier. Hauerwas and William Willimon popularized the notion of "resident aliens" in their two popular books *Resident Aliens: Life in the Christian Colony* and *Where Resident Aliens Live*.[18] In these volumes, Hauerwas and Willimon present an emphatically post-Constantinian model of the church and Christian ministry. The model is post-Constantinian because it rejects the cultural and political arrangement which has existed in the West since the Roman emperor Constantine made Christianity the "official" religion of the Roman Empire. Most often the church has been enthralled with this so-called official status—whether such status is de jure official (as in the case of a state church, like the Anglican faith in

---

[16]Richard John Neuhaus, "Introduction," *First Things* 67 (November 1996): 20.
[17]Charles W. Colson, "Kingdoms in Conflict," *First Things* 67 (November 1996): 35.
[18]Stanley Hauerwas and William Willimon, *Resident Aliens: Life in the Christian Colony* (Nashville: Abingdon, 1991); *Where Resident Aliens Live* (Nashville: Abingdon, 1996).

Britain) or is only de facto official (as in the case of Southern Baptists in the American South). This cultural and political arrangement is delusory not only because it leads the church to endorse national projects that are at odds with the mission of the church (like war) but also because it encourages the church to understand itself, its role and its mission in relation to the identity of the nation. To deny Constantinian Christianity (as Hauerwas and Willimon do) is to affirm that the church's role is other than providing a religious justification for the culture and government of the West.

If the Constantinian model is aptly summed up in the common (but rarely justified) cliché that "one cannot be a good Christian without being a good citizen," then the post-Constantinian model asserts that "one cannot serve two masters." If one's faith primarily serves one's citizenship, then the demands of citizenship dictate the character and practice of whatever is left of religious faith. It is profoundly important to recognize that this model does not denigrate citizenship *qua* citizenship at all. It simply refuses to interpret citizenship under the banner of authentic faith. It refuses to see Christian faith translated into civil religion.

This is not, of course, a philosophy of political retreat. It is a confession of faith about the proper functioning of one's *polis*-ordering commitments. It is thus altogether inaccurate to suggest (as Colson does) that Hauerwas and those who reject the Constantinian picture of the church are "no longer concerned about the fortunes or misfortunes of a flawed republic." They are concerned about the fortunes and misfortunes of the republic, but they do not confuse the fortunes and misfortunes of the republic with those of the church.

And yet it is this inaccurate rendering of Hauerwas that is at the heart of the Notre Dame theology department's rejection of Baxter. Hauerwas is often regarded as affirming a sectarian stance concerning the engagement of religion and politics. The *HarperCollins Encyclopedia of Catholicism*, edited by Richard McBrien, defines *sectarian* as "one who defines the church as the exclusive locus of God's activity, and the mission of the church as limited to a countercultural, otherworldly salvation."[19] Pamela

---

[19]Richard McBrien, ed., *HarperCollins Encyclopedia of Catholicism* (New York: HarperCollins, 1995), p. 1180.

Schaeffer noted in the *National Catholic Reporter* that McBrien

> alluded to his concerns about Hauerwas and his Catholic students in his
> encyclopedia, where he wrote, "Although sectarianism is diametrically op-
> posed to Catholicism, a certain sectarian orientation has emerged in recent
> years in portions of the Catholic peace movement and in some younger
> Catholic moral theologians influenced by Protestant sectarian ethicists."[20]

I will return to this larger issue, but some foreshadowing is perhaps in
order. Alasdair MacIntyre, in his *Three Rival Versions of Moral Enquiry*,
described the "encyclopaedia" approach as one of the three dominant attempts to classify and define moral inquiry.[21] The encyclopedist assumes
an ahistorical posture and attempts to present a clear distinction between
"facts" and "values." The "facts" can be labeled and defined in such a way
so that anyone may simply look up a definition in order to know what a
thing might be. This is the essence of the encyclopedia. The Enlightenment is in many ways exemplified by this quest for definitive representa-
tions. However, if the definition in question turns out to be a contested
one (as most definitions of interesting terms are), the definitive nature of
the encyclopedia is undermined. In the modern context the classic Enlightenment Liberal move is to offer definitions in such a way so as to
preordain the terms (and consequences) of the debate. This phenomenon
is clearly illustrated in the polemical definition of *sectarianism* that appears
in McBrien's *Encyclopedia of Catholicism*.

The entry describes sectarians as "appealing to the individualistic aspects of Christianity,"[22] but that hardly seems the best way to describe
Hauerwas, and certainly not Baxter. Rather than sectarian, Hauerwas's
approach, and that of Baxter, is better described as affirming confessionally particularist approaches to morality, politics and faith. (Their approach is not, however, to be confused with Richard Niebuhr's "confes-
sionalism" in Christian ethics.) Hauerwas grew up a Methodist, Baxter a
Roman Catholic. They differ in that they utilize different resources (and
similar resources in different ways) for addressing the problems presented

---

[20]Schaeffer, "Notre Dame Dispute May Signal a Shift."
[21]Alasdair MacIntyre, *Three Rival Versions of Moral Enquiry* (Notre Dame, Ind.: University of Notre
    Dame, 1990).
[22]McBrien, *HarperCollins Encyclopedia of Catholicism*, p. 1180.

by a moral engagement with politics. They concur in that they affirm that one must employ confessionally particular resources; there are no religiously generic resources. It is safe to say that one of the dreams of Enlightenment Liberalism was the desire to remove the scandal of particularity from the engagement of religion and politics. (It is for this reason that Liberalism will eventually insist on the privatization of religion because historical religions cannot be divorced from their particularities.) Baxter and Hauerwas recognize that the scandal of particularity cannot be removed without compromising authentically Christian convictions.

The term *sectarian* is best known for its use by Ernst Troeltsch (1865-1923) in his 1912 *Social Teachings of the Christian Churches*.[23] Examining the sociology of religious groups, Troeltsch distinguishes the "church" and the "sect" as two of the three principal orientations by which religious groups relate to society and culture. (The third is mysticism.) Troeltsch noted that churches were different from sects in that while churches actively attempt to influence the larger society and culture in which they find themselves, sects withdraw from society and culture—seeking salvation only within the sect. Contemporary sociologists of religion use Troeltsch's typology today in a variety of ways for seeking to understand the role and function of religious groups in our society. The term *sectarian* has thus taken on the pejorative connotations associated with exclusionary religious groups that withdraw from society.

More, however, needs to be said on this matter. One of the problems arising out of this typology is the temptation to confuse "salvation" and "flourishing." The former is an explicitly theological category (usually referring to beliefs about eternal destiny), while the latter is a philosophical one describing the well-being of a particular person or entity. It is of course quite plausible for a religious believer to assert that while all communities that accurately focus their attention on beliefs and practices necessary for salvation are communities within which one finds a robust account of human flourishing, it is not the case that all communities within which one finds a robust account of human flourishing are communities that accurately focus their attention on beliefs and practices necessary for salvation.

---

[23]Ernst Troeltsch, *The Social Teachings of the Christian Churches*, trans. Olive Wyon (Louisville: Westminster/John Knox Press, 1992).

Or in short hand, while all S is F, it is not the case that all F is S.

Many of those groups Troeltsch lists as among the "church" orientation never thought of salvation as something to be acquired outside the church, even though they have worked for the flourishing of the larger society within which they found themselves. The Roman Catholic Church, for instance, has consistently affirmed the principle *extra ecclesium nulla salus* (outside the church there is no salvation), all the while engaging society and the political order, seeking to affect certain goods and outcomes and so forth. In the United States the largely immigrant Roman Catholic Church has never had the "church" status described by Troeltsch, while the quintessentially "sectarian" Southern Baptists have dominated the social and political order of the American South.

All of this calls into question the cavalier way in which "sectarians" are dismissed in McBrien's essay as "appealing to the individualistic aspects of Christianity" and being "diametrically opposed to Catholicism." What is needed to describe Hauerwas and Baxter is a new typology. And for these purposes I have chosen to describe them as *particularist*.

While Neuhaus cannot be described as sectarian (by either Troeltsch's or McBrien's definition), he also recognizes the tension between the confessionally particular and the religiously generic, and the role this tension plays in the debate over the place of religion in the public square. Indeed, the dispute between the generically religious and the particularly Christian is at the heart of the conflict between Gertrude Himmelfarb and Neuhaus, as I will demonstrate later. For the moment, it is enough to see that this tension is exemplified by Neuhaus's increasing recognition of the inadequacy of purely procedural commitments for ensuring the legitimacy of government.[24] The strong commitment to procedure is an Enlightenment move, and it is clearly seen in Himmelfarb's assertion that the legitimacy of government should not be discussed under the rubric of religious commitments, and that the question of the very nature of government is not up for discussion.

Neuhaus and Baxter (and Hauerwas) are in agreement with regard to their dissatisfaction with Himmelfarb here. A point of clarification

---

[24]Richard John Neuhaus, "Anatomy of a Controversy" in *The End of Democracy?* (Dallas: Spence Publishing, 1997).

is in order. Neuhaus, Baxter and Hauerwas are not suggesting alternative forms of government, and contrary to popular opinion Hauerwas does not advocate the modern retreat to Walden Pond (or Ruby Ridge), which might be inferred from Colson's previous comment. (Hauerwas and Thoreau are quite far apart indeed.) But Neuhaus, Baxter and Hauerwas are suggesting (Neuhaus more reluctantly than the others) that not only is it conceivable that "the American experiment in democracy" should fail with respect to its ability either to define an acceptable relationship between religion and the state or to protect religious expression therein defined, but also that politics as reduced to the statecraft of Liberal democracy severely (and from the Christian standpoint, inadequately) limits the possibilities available for "the ordered life of the polis." This is an important point, and it is one to which I shall return.

Make no mistake: Baxter and Neuhaus disagree on many things. They differ with regard to national economic policy as well as national military policy. This latter difference is exemplified by their contrasting opinions on the First Gulf War.[25] They perhaps differ with regard to how moral convictions inform theology (and vice versa). This alleged difference was articulated in print by Neuhaus. In the April 1997 issue of *First Things*, Neuhaus offered a critique of what he took to be Baxter's use of pacifism as the lens through which Christian theology should be viewed. Even though Neuhaus acknowledges that Baxter is "philosophically and theologically light years removed from Kant," he described Baxter's approach as an instance of Kantian "religion within the limits of morality." Neuhaus, describing Baxter as "a modern theologian who critiques the entirety of the tradition by a criterion of his own choosing," cautions his readers against accepting modern moralisms that make claims about the "essence of Christianity." According to Neuhaus,

> Whenever you hear a theologian speak about "the essence" of Christianity, he is probably promoting something other than Christianity. Christianity is not an essence or principle but the story of the world, and is composed of

---

[25]Baxter and Hauerwas affirm similar versions of pacifism. For their differences with Neuhaus on the Gulf War, see Stanley Hauerwas and Richard John Neuhaus, "Pacifism, Just War, and the Gulf," *First Things* 13 (May 1991): 39-45.

the inconvenient historical particularities of God's revelation of Himself in Israel and the Church.[26]

In the August-September 1997 issue of *First Things*, Baxter responded to Neuhaus by denying that the article Neuhaus had critiqued was premised, as Neuhaus had claimed, on a Kantian understanding of the relation between the church and morality. According to Baxter,

> Kant's project was to free morality from tutelage to the authority and tradition of the Church by providing an account of the autonomy of morality grounded in reason qua reason. My article is part of an attempt to demonstrate the necessity of the Church for moral reflection, and the inextricable relation between ecclesial and moral discourse.[27]

There is more to this conversation between Neuhaus and Baxter, but for the moment what is important is the (joint) rejection of the Enlightenment's neutrality thesis and its correlative commitment to morally and religiously generic forms of discourse. All the differences notwithstanding, Neuhaus and Baxter are both thoroughgoing confessional particularists, and the difference with traditional neoconservative forms of Liberalism is striking.

## THE END OF NEUTRALITY AND A CONFLICT OF FAITHS

While tensions between the supposed theocons and neocons had run deep for some time, the distinctions between them (as well as their connection to what would become the Baxter affair) were obvious on at least one occasion some fourteen months before the End of Democracy? symposium. Gertrude Himmelfarb and Neuhaus, together with James William McClendon of Fuller Theological Seminary and David Solomon (Baxter support signatory) of Notre Dame appeared on stage together at an academic symposium in Waco, Texas, at the inauguration of Robert B. Sloan, the twelfth president of Baylor University.

It is not inappropriate to suggest that McClendon, noted "baptist" theologian, represented a perspective with which Baxter resonates in many

---

[26]Richard John Neuhaus, "Religion Within the Limits of Morality Alone," *First Things* 72 (April 1997): 61, 59.

[27]Michael Baxter, "Correspondence," *First Things* 75 (August-September 1997): 4.

ways. In fact, Baxter has spoken of his great respect for McClendon, "especially McClendon's understanding of the proclamation of the Word as shaping how we see the world." Baxter confesses, "Much of my work has been an attempt to expand on that point by means of a liturgical understanding of proclaiming and reading scripture."[28] In a festschrift for McClendon that Hauerwas coedited, Hauerwas described McClendon as "a master craftsman" who has taught us that "in a world without foundations, all we have is the church. That such is the case is no deficiency since that is all we have ever had or could ever want."[29] (McClendon died October 30, 2000.)

The title of the Baylor symposium was "University, Church, and Society: Traditions in Tension," and Solomon was the moderator. The question of what relation Christians should have to the university is a very different question from that of what relation Christians should have to the government.[30] However, both questions are (inadequately) framed by the procedural and substantial assumptions of Enlightenment Liberalism, and both questions address the complex issue of faith and institutional identity in a context of refusal to accept democracy as the most fundamental reality for the human being.

McClendon spoke first, and his subject was "The Baptist Idea of a University."[31] Arguing that the university has an unpaid moral debt to the church, from whence it has come, McClendon suggested that this debt can only be satisfied if the university gives to society what it has been given by the church. Noting that "moral thinking attends to *practices*," McClendon defined *practices* as "complex traditional human endeavors, carried on by those engaging in them with a view to moral ends whose achievement justifies the practices and fulfills the lives of those so engaged." Agreeing with Jonathan Edwards that morality can express itself better in terms of "beauty" than with the metaphor of "debt," McClendon

---

[28]Michael Baxter, interview by the author, February 3, 1997, South Bend, Indiana.

[29]Stanley Hauerwas, "The Church's One Foundation Is Jesus Christ Our Lord," *Theology Without Foundations: Religious Practice and the Future of Theological Truth*, ed. Stanley Hauerwas, Nancey Murphy and Mark Nation (Nashville: Abingdon, 1994), p. 144.

[30]I personally believe this distinction to be a very important one.

[31]James William McClendon Jr., "The Baptist Idea of a University," presented at the "University, Church, and Society: Traditions in Tension" symposium, Baylor University, September 15, 1995.

argued that by "fitly nurturing its own proper practices," the university not only discovers and progressively repays its moral debt but also answers to and corresponds with the beauty that is "the holiness of redemption, the wholeness of creation, God's holy wholeness."[32]

Himmelfarb offered an essay under the title "The Christian University: A Call to Counterrevolution." The counterrevolution, according to Himmelfarb, is the conservative attempt "to restore and revitalize the traditional academic dogma" against the postmodern dangers which threaten the university. Himmelfarb cited approvingly Matthew Arnold's definition of culture as "the best which has been thought and said in the world." This understanding of culture is important because it betrays her commitment to a supposed neutrality based on the presupposition that the "best" ideas are always the exemplification of a culture's heritage. (The best team always wins the knowledge Olympics.) This notion has become problematic given the increasingly marginalized status of an Enlightenment perspective. If Enlightenment ideals are supplanted by post-Enlightenment (or postmodern) ones, were they really superior? Of course, even to speak in these terms assumes that there is a standard by which one can evaluate (and rank) ideas. Enlightenment proponents (like Himmelfarb) will note that the postmodernists have not "played by the rules"; they have cheated, so to speak, thus one cannot rightfully speak of their "winning" anything.

The issue which is most important for our purposes is Himmelfarb's use of Robert Nisbet's *The Degradation of the Academic Dogma*. Himmelfarb explicitly points to Nisbet's use of religious terminology to describe the revolution that occurred in universities during the 1960s. Himmelfarb notes, "Nisbet reminded them of the 'dogma,' as he called it, that had sustained the university for centuries: the 'faith' (again, this was his word) in reason and knowledge, in the rational, dispassionate search for truth, and in the dissemination of knowledge for the sake of knowledge."[33] Himmelfarb uses this religious terminology throughout her presentation. In speaking of the commitment of the university, she affirms, "Throughout

---

[32]Ibid, p. 3.
[33]Gertrude Himmelfarb, "The Christian University: A Call to Counterrevolution," *First Things* 59 (January 1996): 16-19.

the centuries, the essential dogma—the commitment to truth, knowledge, and objectivity—remained intact." Later, Himmelfarb juxtaposes the new postmodern "unholy Trinity of race, class, and gender" with the traditional "dogma" of "truth, objectivity, and knowledge."

It is not mere coincidence that Himmelfarb should speak of the academic "dogmas" in this way. Himmelfarb's faith in the Enlightenment ideal is profoundly religious. In truth, the Enlightenment commitment to "the rational, dispassionate search for truth, and . . . the dissemination of knowledge for the sake of knowledge" is a kind of religion. More importantly, it is a fundamental religion that requires an absolute faithfulness since it alone possesses the capacity to adjudicate between the irrational excesses of traditional religions. As stated earlier, Enlightenment doctrine is not plagued by the "scandal of particularity" that consumes every historical religion. It is accessible to all and in every place. This rational religion need not necessarily deprecate traditional faiths since it is "neutral" and "dispassionate" with regard to the traditional faiths. Rather, it is "the rational, dispassionate search for truth, and . . . the dissemination of knowledge for the sake of knowledge." Father Neuhaus, of course, practices a different religion.

The third presentation was made by Neuhaus, and the deep tensions between Neuhaus and Himmelfarb could not have been more striking, even if on the surface they identified common enemies and celebrated common causes. Neuhaus offered eleven theses on the idea of the Christian university.[34] The former Lutheran pastor quipped that the audience "will no doubt be grateful that there are not ninety-five theses." The first thesis set Himmelfarb's faith in Enlightenment neutrality in bold relief: "There is no such thing as a university pure and simple." Unequivocally denying the neutrality thesis, Neuhaus continued: "A secular university is not a university pure and simple; it is a secular university. Secular is not a synonym for neutral."

Neuhaus's eighth thesis was "In a Christian university there is no 'role' for religion. Rather, it is within religion—more accurately, it is within the Christian understanding of reality—that everything finds its

---

[34]Richard John Neuhaus, "The Christian University: Eleven Theses," *First Things* 59 (January 1996): 20-22.

role." Neuhaus's clarifying clause ("more accurately, it is within the Christian understanding of reality") is important for two reasons. On the one hand he is rejecting the generic account of religion in favor of a particular (i.e., a Christian) one. On the other hand he (like McClendon here) is recognizing the comprehensive nature of the Christian commitment. Himmelfarb fails to recognize either distinction. In her presentation she had spoken of religious universities as "respectful of religion and of the moral virtues derived from religion." Neuhaus's point is the opposite. Within a Christian university, religion does not occupy a respected role precisely because it is from within that commitment that all else finds its role.

Similarly, the Christian operating in the public square does not respect religion in a way in which the secularist does not. Rather, the Christian is simply a Christian. Whether he or she will be able to consent will ultimately have a material rather than a formal explanation. Himmelfarb assumes that these matters can be decided on formal grounds; indeed, to do otherwise would violate the Enlightenment commitment to neutrality, which is the formal guarantee. To place religious commitment outside of the province of the endeavor itself (whether in a respected or depreciated position) is still to domesticate religion. Himmelfarb mistakenly assumes that "being respectful of religion" will be enough. But this move toward functional religion already entails the privatization and trivialization of specific religious commitments.

However, for Neuhaus, McClendon and Baxter, where the Enlightenment dogmas hold sway, there is always the possibility that the Christian will not be able to consent. In point of fact, when Enlightenment dogma is taken as the arbiter of "acceptable" religious convictions, there can never be a real "separation of church and state" because the principle itself is predicated on the prior establishment of a particular faith, a conflicting dogma.

Robert George made this point to the *Chronicle of Higher Education* about the *First Things* symposium. George notes,

> Our objection is to the idea that liberalism itself is a kind of neutral playing field, as opposed to a substantive theory about human nature, destiny, and dignity. We dispute the idea that liberalism itself is a neutral view that doesn't compete with others. It certainly has the right to compete in the

public square with other philosophies, but it is certainly not given any privileged position by the Constitution.[35]

Baxter and Hauerwas make a similar point about Liberalism (though not about the Constitution) in their essay "The Kingship of Christ," and it is the point that (it seems to me) has brought Neuhaus to a crisis of conviction concerning the political nature of Christian faith. In the original article that was the impetus for this volume, I described Neuhaus as a "reluctant particularist." He did not like that title, and I myself am no longer confident that such is the case.

The difference, of course, is that while Baxter and Hauerwas seem to imply that such could never be otherwise, Neuhaus wishes that such were not the case; indeed, he longs to hold the two sides in respectful tension. This is not to suggest that Neuhaus desires an equilibrium but rather that he thinks that if the state respects the natural law, the areas where Christians will find a conflict of conscience will be limited. This is the hope of traditional natural law theory, especially as it has been articulated by Thomists like Jacques Maritain and Ralph McInerny.

In the meantime, however, traditional natural law theory gets pulled in two directions. It is pulled toward a bland, Liberal secularism of the sort advocated by Himmelfarb, which accepts the contributions of generic religions so long as they do not voice particular concerns or question the all-encompassing Liberal faith. It is also pulled toward Baxter's rich confessional and liturgical particularism, which interprets the natural law only in light of its supernatural origin. This position in the end is much closer to the traditional Thomism of Maritain and McInerny, and this is the position to which Neuhaus is drawn.

The profound differences of Baxter and Neuhaus notwithstanding, both are unwavering in their fidelity to the Christian gospel over and against a modern political agenda, which, though it may affirm many common elements, requires the person of faith and conscience to violate both in the name of procedural rationality and democratic process. While Neuhaus cannot bring himself to emulate Baxter's embrace of "particular-

---

[35]Robert George, cited in Christopher Shea, " 'Natural Law' Theory Is at the Crux of a Nasty Intellectual Debate," *Chronicle of Higher Education*, February 7, 1997, p. A14.

ism," he has become a reluctant belligerent in the clash with an Enlightenment Liberalism of which his own cultural and political conservatism is part and parcel.

As a devout Christian, Neuhaus recognizes that he can have no personal religious agendas. And since Neuhaus agrees with Aristotle that politics is free persons deliberating the question "how ought we order our lives together," Neuhaus's political program is not ultimately about propping up conservatism in general or the Religious Right in particular, though he is pleased when the commitments coalesce. For Neuhaus the question is one of conscience and Christian faith—but not about the creation of a mythical "Christian nation." He has reluctantly found himself in his present role, but it is a role he has not shirked.

*5*

---

# GERTRUDE HIMMELFARB
# AND THE PRIORITY
# OF DEMOCRACY TO
# PHILOSOPHY

RICHARD JOHN NEUHAUS ACKNOWLEDGES that the papers given at the Baylor symposium illustrate a fundamental difference between his position and that of Gertrude Himmelfarb. He confesses, however, that he does "want to view Himmelfarb and people of like mind as allies." He notes, "In fact, they are allies on most of the questions currently contested in our public life."[1] Whether this is true depends on at least two qualifications: what it means to be "of like mind" with Gertrude Himmelfarb, and what the most pressing current problems are. According to Neuhaus, I am wrong to suggest that he is "being 'reluctantly' forced to recognize that they are not allies because they are operating on liberal presuppositions that are in irreconcilable conflict with the Christian construal of reality." As I noted in chapter four, I probably was wrong about certain aspects of his "reluctance"; how-

---

[1]Richard John Neuhaus, "The Extraordinary Politics of Alien Citizens," *First Things* 84 (June-July 1998): 61.

ever, I do believe that Gertrude Himmelfarb (and "people of like mind") represent a perspective that is deeply problematic for Christians to affirm.

In what follows I want to suggest that neoconservatives like Himmelfarb and Norman Podhoretz share three crucial assumptions with Liberals like the American philosopher Richard Rorty (who died June 8, 2007). First, they understand religion (or in Rorty's case, the religious impulse) in principally functional and utilitarian terms. Second, they believe that when religion deviates from this functional capacity (for instance, as informing public and political practice) it becomes a "conversation-stopper" and a threat to democracy. Third, and most important, they affirm what Rorty has called "the priority of democracy to philosophy."[2] Taken together, these three deadly assumptions exemplify the reduction of politics to statecraft. In chapters six and seven I will argue that Christians must not only recognize the peril presented by these three deadly assumptions but also enact an extraordinary politics. Such an extraordinary politics must offer a compelling alternative to the hegemony of Enlightenment Liberalism, which these assumptions currently establish. In this chapter I will address these three deadly assumptions by concentrating on Himmelfarb (and speaking only briefly about Rorty and Podhoretz) and contrasting her affirmation of democracy with the more qualified affirmation proposed by John Paul II in his encyclicals. In chapter six I turn to the problematic notion of the reduction of politics to statecraft.

It seems to me that when Father Neuhaus speaks of the "questions currently contested in our public life," he has a variety of very specific public policy issues in mind. Perhaps on matters like abortion, euthanasia, pornography and sexual promiscuity, Himmelfarb and "people of like mind" are allies with Christians like Neuhaus. But on the more foundational issues like the assumptions raised earlier, Himmelfarb finds herself allied with a surprising group of "people of like mind." A close examination of her fundamental commitments concerning democracy, human maturity, justice and the role of faith in a Liberal society reveals that Himmelfarb is far closer to Richard Rorty than to Richard Neuhaus.

---

[2]Richard Rorty, "The Priority of Democracy to Philosophy," *Objectivity, Relativism, and Truth* (Cambridge: Cambridge University Press, 1991).

## RORTY AND HIMMELFARB: UNLIKELY COMPATRIOTS

When Richard Rorty speaks of the "priority of democracy to philosophy," he is claiming that Liberal democracy does not need philosophical justification. This is not only the belief that one's commitments to democracy substantially inform all inquiry into the nature of human flourishing but also the belief that democratic values trump any truth claims (whether from philosophy, religion or any other form of inquiry) that might call democracy into question. Democracy is not "on the table" for discussion; rather, according to Rorty, democracy creates the "table" and makes reasonable discussion possible.

Rorty is far less complimentary of religion than Himmelfarb (or Podhoretz). In the spirit of John Dewey, he values the religious "impulse" insofar as it guarantees a "common faith" in democracy and democratic practice. To this extent, then, Rorty also has a "functional" view of religion. However, Rorty recognizes that religion frequently "functions" in such a way as to undermine democratic values, and thus he is inclined to view religion as a "conversation-stopper." The phrase "religion as a conversation-stopper" comes from Rorty's now famous review of Stephen Carter's *The Culture of Disbelief*, originally published in *Common Knowledge*.[3] Rorty defended the Jeffersonian compromise that privatized religion, kept it out of the public square and made it "seem bad taste to bring religion into discussions of public policy."

For Rorty it is important that one recognize that bringing religion into discussions of public policy should seem to be in bad taste rather than being "philosophically unjustifiable." Rorty recognizes that in a multicultural world dominated by identity politics, it is exceedingly difficult to justify the exclusion of religious claims and insights. But this is not a cause for concern. If one is committed to the priority of democracy to philosophy, one need not have a theory about how religion "fits into" the public square. If religion can contribute to the conversation, fine. But the conversation is democracy—procedural, participatory and anti-authoritarian. The insertion of religious authorities and religious appeals to insight or truth in this conversation is in bad taste because it stops the

---

[3]Richard Rorty, "Religion as Conversation-Stopper," *Common Knowledge* 3 (Spring 1994).

conversation. In reply to a claim that abortion is wrong because it violates God's will, Rorty asks, "Are we atheists supposed to try to keep the conversation going by saying, 'Gee! I'm impressed. You must have a really deep, sincere faith'? Suppose we try that. What happens then? What can either party do for an encore?"[4]

At first glance, it might seem difficult to pair Richard Rorty and Gertrude Himmelfarb on matters of political philosophy and public policy. As public intellectuals these two thinkers are standard-bearers for their respective liberal and conservative causes and seem to personify opposite points of view. Moreover, surely it is the case that they would have opposed one another on many specific issues currently under debate within the public square. Himmelfarb even singled out Rorty for critique. According to Himmelfarb, "We can look into Rorty and see him not as he sees himself—as the only sensible, pragmatic philosopher of liberal democracy—but as the proponent of a relativism-cum-aestheticism that verges on nihilism and that may ultimately subvert liberal democracy."[5]

It should be clear in this quotation that Himmelfarb desires to save Liberal democracy from one who would claim to exemplify its causes. What will become clear is the recognition that for both of them Liberal democracy is the most important and foundational reality confronting the human being today. It is the only appropriate object of public affection and the only legitimate source of, to use Cavanaugh's phrase, our lethal loyalties. On this much, Rorty and Himmelfarb agree.

Given Rorty's sometimes forceful defense of atheism, reflective Christians might be inclined to affirm with Neuhaus that Himmelfarb is an ally "on most of the questions currently contested in our public life." And yet, her differences with Rorty notwithstanding, Himmelfarb affirms with him the centrality of these three deadly assumptions: religion as functional aid to democracy, religion as a conversation-stopper within democracy, and the priority of democracy to philosophy, religion or any competing alternative.

Himmelfarb's views and the temptation she presents to Christians can

---

[4]Ibid., p. 3.
[5]Gertrude Himmelfarb, *On Looking into the Abyss: Untimely Thoughts on Culture and Society* (New York: Vintage Books, 1994), p. 17.

be clearly seen in her 1999 book, *One Nation, Two Cultures*.[6] In many respects *One Nation, Two Cultures* is quite helpful. Subtitled *A Searching Examination of American Society in the Aftermath of Our Cultural Revolution*, the book focuses on the clash between the "dominant culture" of journalism, entertainment and academia and the "dissident culture" that continues to affirm the traditional ideals of family, sexual morality, privacy and patriotism. Most helpful is Himmelfarb's treatment of various social issues: the detrimental effect of government-sponsored child and adult daycare, the disillusionment of dual-career liberation, the crises of both children without fathers and (because of declining birth rates in the West) children without kinfolk. Perhaps these are the sorts of contested questions of our public life that Neuhaus thinks make her an ally with Christians. Surely many Christians will read the book in this way, and it is clear that she sees religious people as fighting for the "values" of her dissident but patriotic culture. Unfortunately, the book fails for Christians because of its fundamental misunderstanding of the genuinely dissident character of what counts as "human flourishing" for the Christian (life in Christ and the church). The failure is all the more tragic in light of how much she gets right.

Himmelfarb argues aggressively for the thesis that in the wake of the recent cultural revolution (a term she reluctantly employs), it is not enough to restore civil society. "It is also necessary to reform and remoralize its institutions" (p. 44). For instance, Himmelfarb wants to create "a moral climate more conducive to a healthy family." She cites as examples:

> where motherhood and domesticity are as respectable as the profession of law or the practice of business; fatherhood (present not absent fatherhood) is identified with manhood; sexual promiscuity is as socially unacceptable as smoking; the "bourgeois" family is an object of esteem rather than derision; and the culture is not deluded by the familiar euphemisms that dignify out-of-wedlock birth as an "alternative mode of parenting," or cohabitation as a "relationship," or an unmarried mate as a "significant other." (p. 58)

With the exception of her desire to see the "bourgeois" family as an

---

[6]Gertrude Himmelfarb, *One Nation, Two Cultures* (New York: Knopf, 1999). Parenthetical references in this chapter refer to this text.

"object of esteem rather derision," I concur with every point, but the "bourgeois" reference masks an important difference. In common parlance, *bourgeois* has become an almost completely equivocal term. For Himmelfarb the reference to the bourgeois family is conceptual cover for a certain picture of social stability that is achieved through financial prosperity. Since this is the case, it is not surprising that she returns, over and over again, to models of economic prosperity and individual independence as the paradigms of human success and flourishing.

For Himmelfarb religion and religious believers can make an important contribution to the "reforming" and "remoralizing" of the civil society. Throughout *One Nation*, she trumpets the value of functional religion as an "indispensable" foundation to a healthy American democracy. She notes that the "practice of religion has a high correlation with family stability, communal activity, and charitable contributions and a low correlation with suicide, depression, drug addiction, alcoholism, and crime" (p. 95). Religion is even "conducive to physical well-being" since "regular church attendance is correlated with a stronger immune system and lower morality rates from heart, liver, and lung diseases" (p. 95).

Many Christians will read these words and rejoice. And, if regular church attendance makes a positive contribution to my immune system, that's wonderful news. It is not, of course, the reason why one goes to church, and understanding religion in these functional categories places one in direct contradiction to historic Christianity (and Judaism and Islam for that matter).

Himmelfarb, remember, is interested in "creating a moral climate" and in "reforming and remoralizing [civil] institutions." How should such a remoralization occur? What priorities will structure this new reformation? What institutions are competent to create a "moral climate"? For Himmelfarb the desired moral climate is one in which the nation-state shapes the character of free, autonomous individuals whose only consuming allegiance is to this otherwise liberating nation-state. Such a conclusion is surely regrettable and ironic for one like Himmelfarb who has frequently cautioned against the abuses of the state and the delusions of the individual. And yet no authority can genuinely stand before these gods, and she herself has the paved the way for their enthronement.

Concerning the nation-state, she strongly believes that "statecraft is a form of soulcraft" (p. 83). Relying on George Will's catchy phrase, she believes that statecraft "helps shape the character, and hence the soul, of a people." Himmelfarb believes that we are in danger of losing this basic commitment to statecraft as soulcraft because individuals more and more seek their satisfaction in their families and communities. This is an odd conclusion for one who wants to create a "moral climate more conducive to a healthy family." What we discover is that Himmelfarb believes that a "healthy" family is to be defined as one whose ends are directed toward the goods of bourgeois materialism and a prosperous nation-state. As she notes, it is "natural and commendable" for some to make family and community commitments "the center of their emotional ties and moral commitments." But, she cautions, "to feel completely fulfilled in those roles and entirely identified with them is to lose that larger identity and aspiration that come not from civil society but from the polity" (p. 83). Note that for Himmelfarb the "larger" (more comprehensive) "identity and aspiration" (who we are and what we long to become) must be grounded in the polity of the state—not in our various emotional and moral commitments. She does not tell us whether church is an emotional or a moral commitment.

Concerning the autonomous individual, she wants to argue for the "moral character of work." In *The Demoralization of Society* (1995), she recognizes that "the ethos of a society, its moral and spiritual character, cannot be reduced to economic, material, political, or other factors, that values—or, better yet, virtues—are a determining factor in their own right."[7] But where do these values (or virtues) come from? For Himmelfarb they come from a "powerful ethos" formed in the recognition that "self-help" and "self-discipline" create community, "neighbourliness" and philanthropy. She cites Adam Smith and notes that "self-discipline and self-control were thought of as the source of self-respect and self-betterment; and self-respect is the precondition for the respect and approbation of others."[8]

What are the consequences for this view of self-betterment as moral

---

[7]Gertrude Himmelfarb, *The Demoralization of Society: From Victorian Virtues to Modern Values* (New York: Alfred A. Knopf, 1995), p. 257.
[8]Ibid., p. 256.

climate? It means that a self-disciplined bourgeois citizen can give thanks to the only gods that matter—a country and a market economy that have made the "good life" possible. Such consequences are succinctly, if offensively, expressed by another who is "of like mind" with Gertrude Himmelfarb, Norman Podhoretz. Published in 2000, Podhoretz's *My Love Affair with America: The Cautionary Tale of a Cheerful Conservative* is rife with praise and gratitude for the functional religion of self-betterment, but he takes matters one step further.

Podhoretz begins the concluding chapter of his book by asserting, "In the end, I suppose, it all comes down to gratitude."[9] Thanks to "this habit of giving thanks," his "spiritual and intellectual immune system was stronger than ever."[10] (Presumably a variety of practices contribute to the health of our immune systems.) Podhoretz gives thanks to America. And while he explicitly denies that America is God, this denial is merely a de jure distinction. De facto, America and the Constitution function as the only deity to whom one must respond. Podhoretz subverts the traditional Jewish *dayyenu*, the concluding word of gratitude spoken in Jewish prayer which expresses the notion that while "that alone would have been enough for us," God has provided more. Podhoretz gives thanks to America for the Constitution, for "domestic tranquility" and for the "common defense that has kept our homeland safe." He writes, "Any one of these blessings would have been enough, but America gave us all of them together."[11]

The book ends with an appalling "American-style dayyenu" in which Podhoretz expresses gratitude to his god America for his Manhattan apartment, for giving him *Commentary* magazine, for enabling him to "mingle with interesting people" and for his big country house on the East End of Long Island. If this testimonial to consumerism were not so tragic, it would be hilarious.

Richard Rorty, of course, abhors the neoconservative politics of Podhoretz and Himmelfarb, and yet, more candidly than they, he expresses the same de facto replacement of God with America. According to Rorty, America is "the first nation-state with nobody but itself to please—not

---

[9]Norman Podhoretz, *My Love Affair with America* (New York: Free Press, 2000), p. 187.
[10]Ibid., p. 192.
[11]Ibid., p. 233.

even God. We are the greatest poem because we put ourselves in the place of God. . . . Other nations thought of themselves as hymns to the glory of God. We redefine God as our future selves."[12]

Himmelfarb would never put it in quite these terms, but her functional view of religion entails just this creation of a new religion. Protest though she may, she too is antecedently committed to William James's belief (enthusiastically endorsed by Rorty) that "democracy is a kind of religion, and we are bound not to admit its failure. Faiths and utopias are the noblest exercise of human reason, and no one with a spark of reason in him will sit down fatalistically before the croaker's picture."[13]

Throughout *One Nation*, Himmelfarb offers comforting words to secularists that religious folk serve many noble purposes and really should not be feared. At the end of the volume she predicts that religious groups will focus on moral rather than religious ideals, and all to the betterment of democracy. She notes, "As religious groups begin to feel more self-confident and less beleaguered, they tend to shed some of their sectarianism and intransigence" (p. 143). Religion *qua* morality is acceptable (provided that they act like mature, rational, secular beings). Religion *qua* religion is a conversation-stopper.

## HIMMELFARB AND *FIRST THINGS*

This perspective was already evident in Himmelfarb's vociferous response to the *First Things* symposium. She responded in print to the *First Things* symposium several times, including her letter of resignation to the *First Things* editorial board, a letter to the *American Spectator* and her contribution to the *Commentary* symposium. In her letter of resignation (printed in *First Things*, January 1997), she expressed her agreement with the symposium participants in their conviction that the courts had overstepped their bounds, but she strongly disagreed with the notion that such a conclusion warrants questioning the legitimacy of the government. She found that it was "absurd and irresponsible" to suggest an analogy between the "revolu-

---

[12]Richard Rorty, *Achieving Our Country* (Cambridge, Mass.: Harvard University Press, 1998), p. 22.

[13]William James, "The Social Value of the College-Bred," in James, *Essays, Comments, and Reviews* (Cambridge, Mass.: Harvard University Press, 1987), p. 109, cited in Rorty, *Achieving Our Country*, p. 9.

tionary" situations of 1776 and the present day. She objected to the use of
the word *regime*, for such "suggests that it is not the legitimacy of a particular institution or branch of government that is at stake but the very
nature of our government." For Himmelfarb, as already noted, this is not
"a proper mode of political discourse." In effect Himmelfarb is arguing
not only that the legitimacy of government should not be discussed under
the rubric of religious commitments and morality but also that the question of the very nature of government is not up for discussion or philosophical speculation. This, of course, is Rorty's position exactly—the priority of democracy to philosophy.

Himmelfarb amplified these comments in her longer contribution to
*Commentary*'s February 1997 symposium. Here she also began by contrasting the now distant "Gingrich revolution" of 1994 with the specter of
revolution behind the *First Things* symposium, but again quickly noted
that talk about "revolution" is not "a proper mode of conservative discourse
or politics."[14]

In Himmelfarb's opinion, it is when the *First Things* editors cite the
"authority of Western civilization and two papal encyclicals" to sanction
that "laws which violate the moral law are null and void and must in conscience be disobeyed" that their argument becomes confused. She is quite
frankly shocked and dismayed at this line of reasoning. It is understandable that Himmelfarb would be confused at this point because she is using
the converse of the hermeneutical principle employed by the *First Things*
editors. For some of them "Western civilization" is interpreted in the light
of the encyclicals; for Himmelfarb, it has to be the other way around.

But Himmelfarb misunderstands the confusion. She takes the "real issue" to be "abortion and euthanasia."[15] Himmelfarb goes on to speculate
how the *First Things* editors would respond if the legalization of abortion
had come through the legislature instead of the judiciary: "If it betokened
not the 'end of democracy' but the very exercise of democracy."

Essential to the Enlightenment Liberal culture is a claim to advocacy
of a procedural "come what may." Himmelfarb makes precisely this point.
She writes, "If conservatives do take democracy and the Constitution seri-

---

[14]Gertrude Himmelfarb, "On the Future of Conservatism," *Commentary*, February 1997, p. 30.
[15]Ibid., p. 31.

ously, if we are truly exercised by the usurpation of judicial power, we must also be prepared for the possibility that *vox populi* might differ from many of us on the subject of abortion." Whereas Neuhaus interprets the "legal" in light of the "moral," Himmelfarb does the opposite. According to Himmelfarb, those who disagree with the properly procedural implications of democracy, "have neither the moral nor the legal right, in the name of democracy, to impose their view upon the polity, any more than the judiciary today has that right."[16]

Surely Himmelfarb has missed the point. Neuhaus and company were arguing that until recently, the consent of the governed was not in question. Recent judicial actions have called that consent into question. Nowhere does Neuhaus (or by extension, Baxter) suggest that his view should be imposed on the polity. Neuhaus's view is that the repeated violation of conscience makes the question of consent problematic.

The objective of Himmelfarb's article is to demonstrate that the *First Things* symposium places the delicate alliance of "economic conservatives and social conservatives, evangelicals and secularists, federalists, pro-lifers, flat-taxers, and a variety of one-issue partisans" in peril. Surely Neuhaus regrets such a consequence, but it is equally the case that such is obviously beside the point. The theocons and Baxter have taken the positions they have on the basis of principle—not on the basis of procedural politics. Thus all the *Commentary* authors' complaints about how the *First Things* symposium hurts national conservative politics is both true and trivial. The symposium was never about sustaining or affirming a national conservative agenda; had it been so, it would have been the contradiction in terms its critics lamented. More to the point and as noted earlier, if the *First Things* symposium was merely about affirming a traditional conservative political agenda, it could never have existed.

Neuhaus confirms this analysis in "The Anatomy of a Controversy." As his insightful eighty-page essay draws to a close, Neuhaus affirms,

> The argument at the heart of the matter does not most importantly have to do with constitutional interpretation, and certainly not with gyrations within the "the conservative movement." At the heart of the matter is the

---

[16]Ibid.

proposition that we are not God, that God is God. The present controversy reveals once again how our public discourse is disinclined to engage seriously the implications of such a proposition.[17]

Neuhaus notes how much of the cultural, media and academic establishment views phrases from the Pledge of Allegiance such as "under God" as "pious rhetorical embellishment" or "empty flourishes." According to Neuhaus, "The political, cultural, moral, and spiritual crisis of our country is that those who dominate our public discourse, whether on the left or on the right, are unwilling, and perhaps incapable, of acknowledging a higher authority than procedural rules and partisan agendas."[18] Here any unwillingness certainly arises from a genuine inability to understand, and thus charitably engage, the conceptual issues at stake. The discourse of politics which understands commitment to country as radically (literally, "from the root") subservient to commitment to one's God violates a fundamental principle of Liberal political rationality. Such a position is understood as "nonsense" precisely because Liberalism can make "no sense" out of such a hierarchy of commitments. Liberalism, whether in its Himmelfarb or Rorty guise, must insist on the priority of democracy to philosophy. The scandalous hierarchy of commitments is what the *First Things* editors meant by religion as a "subversive force" in the follow-up January 1997 editorial and elsewhere.

And yet the neoconservative critics of the symposium consistently demonstrated how poorly they understood the issues that were (and are) at stake. Four years after the symposium, Norman Podhoretz continued to carp about *First Things*'s "dangerous extremism" in *My Love Affair with America*. As noted earlier, Podhoretz believes that amid America's many problems, one is obliged to be grateful. And though Podhoretz puts a theological spin on thankfulness (gratitude is "at the very center of Judaism, which requires the observant Jew to thank God so often it is a wonder he has time for anything else"),[19] it is quite clear that it is not God but America to whom Podhoretz gives thanks.

---

[17]Richard John Neuhaus, "The Anatomy of a Controversy," in *The End of Democracy? The Judicial Usurpation of Politics* (Dallas: Spence Publishing, 1997), pp. 242-43.

[18]Ibid., pp. 243, 244.

[19]Podhoretz, *My Love Affair with America*, p. 187.

Baxter has presented the case in even more stark terms, and he has little interest in arguing for the Pledge of Allegiance—with, without or under God. As Alfred Freddoso noted, "Baxter has forcefully articulated the position that there is an inherent tension between the demands of Christian witness and the founding principles of the American polity, with the result that Christian witness in the American context will inevitably be counter-cultural." It is precisely the founding principles of this polity which thoroughgoing Liberals like Himmelfarb and Rorty refuse to subject to scrutiny. According to Himmelfarb and "people of like mind," the founding principles of the American polity are immune to scrutiny because they assume that the political and economic realms can be separated from the spiritual realm. While such a separation is entirely consistent with the culture of Enlightenment Liberalism, it is not acceptable from an historically Christian position, as recent papal encyclicals have demonstrated.

## JOHN PAUL II AND DEMOCRACY'S "EMPTY WORD"

Pope John Paul II has been more than willing to subject these principles of Enlightenment Liberalism to scrutiny. John Paul II's *Centesimus Annus* (1991) celebrates the hundredth anniversary, and follows the tradition, of Leo XIII's *Rerum Novarum*, which challenged the Liberal notion that economics is determined exclusively by its own laws and processes. Stanley Hauerwas, in an essay titled "In Praise of *Centesimus Annus*," notes that *Rerum Novarum* sought to undermine this alleged independence of economics by making a worker's just wage "*the* criterion for good economic relations. For the 'just wage' is determined by calculating what is required for the sustaining of families and children, not by the exigencies of the autonomous market."[20]

*Centesimus Annus* focuses on the extraordinary changes that occurred in the world in 1989, not the least of which was the collapse of the communist states and their collectivist economies. Thus while *Centesimus Annus* celebrates the progress and the potential of democracy over totalitarian regimes it also explicitly rejects the neoconservative assumption that eco-

---

[20]Stanley Hauerwas, "In Praise of *Centesimus Annus*," in *In Good Company: The Church as Polis* (Notre Dame, Ind.: University of Notre Dame Press, 1996), p. 128.

nomics can be separated from the spiritual realm. Noting that the "modern business economy has positive aspects," John Paul II asserts that economic activity "includes the right of freedom as well as the duty of making responsible use of freedom." And later, "Economic freedom is only one element of human freedom."[21] This responsible use of freedom includes a recognition of the moral character of work. But John Paul II's notion of the "moral character of work" strikes a profound contrast with the same notion in Himmelfarb. In the place of self-betterment as the precondition for the approbation of others, John Paul II writes, "It is becoming clearer how a person's work is naturally interrelated with the work of others. More than ever, work is work with others and work for others: It is a matter of doing something for someone else."[22] Later, I will explore how the practice of hospitality exemplifies this work with others and work for others.

Neoconservatives have often downplayed the fact that life and work in a capitalist economy does indeed have a communally recognized spiritual dimension. John Paul II leaves no doubt where the Christian tradition stands on this matter:

> Even prior to the logic of a fair exchange of goods and the forms of justice appropriate to it, there exists *something which is due to the person because he is a person*, by reason of his lofty dignity. Inseparable from that required "something" is the possibility to survive and, at the same time, to make an active contribution to the common good of humanity.[23]

In *Evangelium Vitae* (1995), John Paul II's endorsement of democracy became even more qualified. As such, the pope has amplified his comments by affirming that there is more to the moral life than talk about democratic and economic rights. For John Paul II a democracy worthy of the name must recognize the value of human life.

> Democracy cannot be idolized to the point of making it a substitute for morality or a panacea for immorality. Fundamentally, democracy is a "system" and as such is a means and not an end. Its "moral" value is not automatic, but depends on conformity to the moral law.[24]

---

[21]*Centesimus Annus*, pp. 32, 39.
[22]Ibid., p. 31.
[23]Ibid., p. 34.
[24]*Evangelium Vitae*, p. 70.

Both Baxter and Neuhaus are responding in accordance with John Paul II's insight that Enlightenment Liberalism's regulation of difference through mere procedural rationality is not sufficient. Democracy as "a mere mechanism for regulating different and opposing interests" is not a moral justification. According to John Paul II,

> Peace which is not built upon the values of the dignity of every individual and of solidarity between all people frequently proves to be illusory. Even in participatory systems of government, the regulation of interests often occurs to the advantage of the most powerful, since they are the ones most capable of maneuvering not only the levers of power but also of shaping the formation of consensus. In such a situation, democracy easily becomes an empty word.[25]

Neither Gertrude Himmelfarb nor Norman Podhoretz (and Richard Rorty) could ever affirm this language or the ideas it expresses because it allows discussion on "the very nature of our government." Democracy for Himmelfarb and those of like mind can never become an empty word.

## CONCLUSION

The extraordinary politics suggested in this volume does not desire the overthrow of American democracy and the denial of the many goods and privileges which have come in its wake. Extraordinary politics, following Kuhn's metaphor discussed in chapter one, is merely politics that is directed toward different ends and under rival assumptions from those of Liberal democracy. Such an alternative politics is committed to reminding Christians that America is not the most important political issue, democracy is a means to an end, and the Christian faith does not rise or fall with the fortunes of democratic Liberalism or the United States of America.

Indeed, in the current cultural context we Christians will find ourselves set against Enlightenment Liberalism more often than not. For the church, there is an essential connection between "conversation" and "contemplation." Aristotle recognized that genuine friendship based on a common conception of the Good is necessary for contemplation to flourish.[26]

---

[25]Ibid.
[26]Aristotle *Nicomachean Ethics* bks. 8-10.

The Himmelfarb and Rorty protest against religion as a conversation-stopper turns out ultimately to be a protest against communal faith as the impetus for contemplation.

The issue is not religion as a conversation-stopper. "Religion" as the name for a collection of privately held beliefs and emotive intuitions is essentially harmless. The real conversation-stopper for Himmelfarb and people of like mind, like Podhoretz and Rorty, is a faith that is not content to be merely penultimate commitment. Faith as ultimate commitment denies the priority of democracy to philosophy and denies that politics and soulcraft can ever be satisfactorily reduced to statecraft.

# 6

## *SAPERE AUDE!*

### From Liberal Statecraft to Extraordinary Politics

IN THIS CHAPTER I TURN TO THE QUESTION of the "reduction of politics to statecraft." The crucial issue here is one of competing conceptions of human flourishing, and with that, the nature of human maturity. Extraordinary politics is predicated on different conceptions of what it means to be mature and what counts as human flourishing. Because the Christian *polis* produces a different sort of person, the politics of such a *polis* will be different as well. The Enlightenment notion of maturity comes to us principally from Immanuel Kant and is exemplified in Max Weber. Both Kant and Weber demand that their readers "grow up" and "be realistic" about the prospects for human futures and possibilities for politics and truth. Kant challenges his readers with a quotation from Horace, *"Sapere aude!"*—usually translated as "Dare to know!" or "Have the courage to use your own understanding!"[1]

---

[1]Immanuel Kant, "An Answer to the Question: 'What Is Enlightenment?' " *Kant: Political Writings*, ed. Hans Reiss, trans. H. B. Nisbet, 2nd ed. (Cambridge: Cambridge University Press, 1991), p. 54.

Here I challenge Kant's understanding of Horace and the incumbent picture of human maturity it fosters. I reject the notion that all politics is best understood through the rubric of the modern nation-state (statecraft) and argue that a proper exercise of politics is a formation of persons (soulcraft) that calls into question the hegemony of Liberalism and the modern nation-state.

Defining *Liberalism* turns out to be a difficult endeavor. Though I have already offered one interpretation, the point I want to emphasize at this juncture is well made by Sandford Lakoff. "Liberalism is not just one of many possible ideologies but nothing less than 'Americanism' itself, the founding ideology that has shaped our way of thinking and our institutions."[2] Christian extraordinary politics rejects "Americanism" as an adequate way to shape our thinking, to develop our institutions or to mold our children and ourselves toward maturity.

Richard John Neuhaus has accused me (with "Hauerwas and Co.") of betraying "a tendency to reify 'liberalism,' turning it into a concrete and coherent doctrine far beyond what many who affirm 'the liberal tradition' recognize as their own position."[3] Perhaps—though I've never suggested Liberalism was coherent. The real question here is not how best to define *Liberalism*. The real question concerns the nature and proper functioning of politics. Is politics merely statecraft, or is there a place in politics for soulcraft as well? Put another way, are there political associations other than the state which contribute to the ordering of our lives together and make substantive contributions to the formation and maturation of our souls? Surely this is the case. Families, churches, synagogues, mosques, neighborhoods, organized groups of coworkers (like trade unions or academic departments in a university) and even "lifestyle enclaves" count as formative political associations.[4] While Robert Bellah and his colleagues have amply demonstrated that not all of these groups have the capacity or

---

[2]Sandford Lakoff, "The Threat of Community," *Review of Politics* 58, no 4 (1996): 809-10.

[3]Richard John Neuhaus, "The Extraordinary Politics of Alien Citizens," *First Things* 84 (June-July 1998): 61.

[4]Robert Bellah and colleagues coined the phrase "lifestyle enclaves" to identify groups of people whose association is based on some activity or interests which binds them together. In Robert Bellah lifestyle enclaves are distinguished from communities of memory (*Habits of the Heart* [New York: Harper & Row, 1985]).

the resources to enable their communities to create and sustain morally coherent lives, it should be obvious that these associations do order our lives in the *polis* and frequently play important (and unequal) roles in the formation of who we are.

When we assume that each of these associations ought to be run in the way that the modern nation-state is run, when we use the vocabularies and the ideas proper to statecraft to structure and develop these associations, then we have reduced politics to statecraft. When we assume (as is frequently the case) that the only legitimate government is a certain sort of democratic one, then politics is reduced even further to a very specific type of statecraft.

I imagine two objections to this assertion might immediately arise. The first objection is that it simply is not the case that there is significant cultural demand that associations such as the ones I have noted should be run like modern nation-states. Clearly I believe this counter-assertion to be false and will attempt to demonstrate that. The second objection takes umbrage at the implied critique of democracy and asks what alternative to democratic government I would suggest. This is an important objection, but I believe it betrays a misunderstanding of my project and should be addressed directly.

Though in common parlance we use the words *government* and *politics* interchangeably, my thesis depends on distinguishing between them. As noted in the introduction, *government* is connotative of what I am calling "statecraft." Our Enlightenment Liberal context repeatedly tells us that the obvious goal of politics is to control the government. I reject that assumption. Controlling the government (statecraft) is one dimension of the ordered life of the *polis*, but it is far from obvious that it is the most important dimension. The ordered life of the *polis* is also the basis for the formation and maturation of persons, souls in this common moral life. My contention (and it is hardly mine alone) is that we should not be limited in our formation of persons to the ways we form and govern nation-states. It seems that such should be obvious, but it has been frequently forgotten.

Theoretically, my goal is to emphasize that there is more conceptual space in the notion of politics than there is in statecraft. I have nothing against statecraft—even Liberal statecraft. As I have already acknowledged, understood as statecraft, Liberal democracy is unmatched, and it is certainly superior to much of what has preceded it. But as soulcraft, Liberalism is woefully inadequate for the formation of persons who have competing ideas about and practices for obtaining human maturity.

The question "What's your alternative to democracy?" misses the point because my complaint is not with statecraft *qua* statecraft. My complaint is with politics *qua* statecraft and with Christians who refuse to see the difference. I want to address that dimension of politics that includes soulcraft, and unlike George Will, Gertrude Himmelfarb, Richard Rorty and Martha Nussbaum, I unequivocally reject the proposition that statecraft makes for adequate soulcraft.[5] Soulcraft must be predicated on a particular *telos* or goal for human maturity. The account of human maturity given by the Christian church is radically at odds with the one bequeathed to us from Enlightenment Liberalism.

In the traditional account of the modern age, soulcraft gets banished from politics and is left to religion, private religion. Religious observers who protest this state of affairs are accused of desiring to replace democracy with theocracy. (Some Christians—especially some conservative Christians—actually think theocracy is possible and, if possible, desirable. I disagree. I find it hard to imagine what a persuasive account of theocratic statecraft would be.) Theocracy is not the issue. The United States of America is not the issue. The issue is human maturity—what it means to be a mature, flourishing human being. How is this to be achieved within the ordered life of the *polis?* Put another way, is there a kind of politics which makes for adequate soulcraft? I believe that there is, but it is not politics as usual. It's really quite extraordinary.

In what follows I want to return to the analogy to Thomas Kuhn's analysis of how scientific revolutions proceed.[6] Kuhn's notion of "paradigm shifts" has become so overused in popular and scholarly works as to border on becoming trite. Rhetorically, however, the analogy does lend

---

[5]George Will, *Statecraft as Soulcraft* (New York: Simon & Schuster, 1983); Gertrude Himmelfarb, *One Nation, Two Cultures* (New York: Knopf, 1999); Richard Rorty, *Achieving Our Country* (Cambridge, Mass.: Harvard University Press, 1998); Martha Nussbaum, *Cultivating Humanity* (Cambridge, Mass.: Harvard University Press, 1997).
[6]Thomas Kuhn, *The Structure of Scientific Revolutions* (Chicago: University of Chicago Press, 1962).

itself well to the more important idea of extraordinary politics.

According to Kuhn, during periods of "normal science" within which there is a single, dominant paradigm ordering scientific research, the activities of science take the form of "puzzle solving." New data is collected and connections between the datum are proposed, tested and confirmed. There are always problems in science that cannot be solved, but as long as these problems are at the margins of inquiry or are dwarfed by more pressing concerns, the dominant paradigm remains unchallenged.

For Kuhn, rival paradigms emerge because the puzzle-solving resources are no longer adequate to meet the challenges of the new day. The emergence of rival paradigms during a period of normal science inaugurates a period of "extraordinary science." Periods of extraordinary science are often chaotic, not only because fundamental assumptions have been called into question but also because any appeal to the "facts" will be inconclusive precisely because the interlocutors cannot agree on what the "facts" are (since to do so would require agreement on interpretative, foundational assumptions). As Stanley Fish has noted, "Disagreements are not settled by the facts, but are the means by which the facts are settled."[7] Making the analogy to politics, Liberalism has been the dominant puzzle-solving paradigm of the West for the last three hundred years, and in the twentieth century has appeared utterly compelling in the face of Nazism, Stalinism and communism.[8]

However, once the Cold War began to wind down and the external challenges to Liberalism receded into the shadows, the internal problems that had been at the margins of Liberal inquiry came to the forefront. In the wake of the loss of our dominant puzzle-solving paradigm, we have the good fortune of being forced to explore alternative models of politics. This is extraordinary politics. In this case, Liberal statecraft is not being called into question. Rather, Liberal statecraft masquerading as soulcraft is what I find so unsatisfactory.

The so-called Liberalism-Communitarianism debate of the 1980s and

---

[7]Stanley Fish, "What Makes an Interpretation Acceptable?" *Is There a Text in This Class?* (Cambridge, Mass.: Harvard University Press, 1980), p. 338.

[8]George Parkin Grant, *English-Speaking Justice* (Notre Dame, Ind.: University of Notre Dame Press, 1985).

1990s was principally about what sort of "souls" Liberalism is competent to produce, and what kind of life we can reasonably expect to live among such souls. The answer, it seems to me, is clear: Liberalism produces an unencumbered self whose highest expression of maturity is the freely willing of one's own will (Kant) that neither infringes upon the rights of others (Mill) nor fails to exercise a realistic ethic of responsibility in a newly disenchanted world (Weber).

To demonstrate that such Enlightenment Liberalism not only is the case but also is committed to reducing all significant politics to responsible, disenchanted statecraft, I need to address two questions: how did this state of affairs come about, and how is this state of affairs manifested in our contemporary political situation? First, I will turn to a brief genealogy of the transformation of maturity as it is found in Hobbes, Kant and Weber. In this narrative Kant is the most important actor. Second, I will illustrate the effects of this arrangement on our contemporary situation by showing how the reduction of politics to statecraft transforms a social institution like marriage through the importation of a certain set of assumptions, vocabularies and procedures.

## HUMAN FLOURISHING AND MATURITY

More than to any other political thinker, Liberalism owes the assumption that politics is reducible to statecraft to the English philosopher and political theorist Thomas Hobbes (1588-1679). Hobbes is best known for his subversive political masterwork, *Leviathan*. First published in 1651, *Leviathan* contains Hobbes's extended argument that science, rather than the nonsense which had been traditionally taught in the schools and practiced in the royal court, should be used to guide the affairs of the commonwealth in all matters, "ecclesiasticall and civil." Such a new "political science" shows that human beings, left to their own natures and in the absence of ruling government, would find themselves in "a war of all against all," producing that famous description of life in the state of nature as "solitary, poor, nasty, brutish, and short."[9]

In the first part of *Leviathan*, Hobbes begins by setting himself against

---

[9]Thomas Hobbes, *Leviathan*, ed. Ewin Curley (Indianapolis: Hackett, 1994), p. 76.

the received philosophical tradition of Aristotle and Thomas Aquinas. Contemplation of the life well-lived is not the highest good for human beings; indeed, Hobbes notes, "For there is no such *Finis ultimus* (utmost aim) nor *Summum Bonum* (greatest good) as is spoken of the books of the old moral philosophers."[10] For Aristotle, contemplation of the life well-lived exemplifies what it means to flourish as a human being. Contemplation is the ultimate means by which our souls are formed in accordance with the Good. Aquinas incorporates the Aristotelian insights into a Christian framework for understanding (contemplating) the goodness of God's creation and God's created gifts. For Thomas this is what it means for human beings, created in the image of God and created for friendship with God, to "flourish."

Hobbes, however, replaces the quest for flourishing with the achievement of prosperity and security. There must be a strong state for there to be public order and therefore security and prosperity. Crucial to Hobbes's argument is his assumption that only the sovereign can bring peace and security, and thus the sovereign must not be forced into alliances that might compete for the ultimate allegiance of the citizen. The nature of the social contract is that there is but one sovereign who can establish prosperity and security. Since no issue is potentially more contentious than religion, religion must itself be brought into the larger service of the state. The church and uniform religious practice is absorbed into the state, and the citizen's ultimate allegiance is to the sovereign, who is the king and supreme pontiff of the realm. In this situation, the church not only loses any sense of its international and ahistorical character, it also forfeits the unique identification and allegiance that formerly attached its members to it.

The arrival of religious toleration did not substantively change this understanding of human success as consisting in security and prosperity precisely because seventeenth-century toleration solidified the identification of politics with statecraft. Politics, as John Locke (1632-1704) understands it, is not about religious ends at all; it is merely about "civic interests." Toleration of religious diversity is not a radical departure from Hobbes's enforcement of uniform practice and belief. As William Cavanaugh notes,

---

[10]Ibid., p. 57.

"Once the state has succeeded in establishing dominance over, or absorbing, the Church, it is but a small step from absolutist enforcement of religious unity to the toleration of religious diversity."[11]

The absorption of the church into the unique and exclusive sovereignty of the state receives its most complete expression in the thought of Immanuel Kant (1724-1804). Moreover, in Kant the very idea of "enlightenment" becomes synonymous with a particular understanding of human maturity.

In Kant's famous essay "An Answer to the Question, 'What Is Enlightenment?' " (1784) Kant argues that enlightenment is emergence from self-imposed immaturity. The immaturity is self-imposed because it arises from a lack of courage to use one's understanding without guidance from another. This immaturity comes easily because the work of thinking is hard. It is easier to buy a book or pay one's pastor or physician for answers to the hard questions than to think for oneself. According to Kant, this immaturity is characteristic of most human beings.[12]

Kant is unclear about the moral culpability of this state of affairs. While it is certainly "self-incurred," the intellectual and political "laziness and cowardice" is perpetuated by the guardians of society who cast fear into the hearts and minds of those who would attempt "to walk alone." Like domesticated animals, the immature souls have become comfortable in depending on the guardians for insight and truth. Intellectual immaturity has become a "second nature." "Dogmas and formulas" have become the "ball and chain of his permanent immaturity." Kant laments that "only a few, by cultivating their own minds, have succeeded in freeing themselves from immaturity and in continuing boldly on their way." To those who have ears to hear, Kant says: "*Sapere aude!* 'Have courage to use your own understanding!' "[13]

One might think that Kant's emphasis on the mature intellectual as a solitary, monological knower would free maturity from a certain captivity to statecraft. For Kant, however, matters are more complicated. Kant dis-

---

[11]William T. Cavanaugh, " 'A Fire Strong Enough to Consume the House:' The Wars of Religion and the Rise of the State," *Modern Theology* 11, no. 4 (1995): 407.
[12]Immanuel Kant, "An Answer to the Question, 'What Is Enlightenment?' " p. 54.
[13]Ibid.

tinguishes between public and private uses of reason. The public use of reason (for instance, "a man of learning addressing the entire reading public") "must always be free, and it alone can bring enlightenment." Private uses of reason are those which one employs in the exercise of a particular office or civil post. Kant believes that private uses of reason may be somewhat restricted without "undue hindrance to the progress of enlightenment." Does this mean that in the interest of the progress of enlightenment the bureaucratic machinery must go on? Such seems to be the case, and Kant, ever the good Prussian, even says as much: "In some affairs which affect the interests of the commonwealth, we require a certain mechanism whereby some members . . . must behave passively. . . . It is, of course, impermissible to argue in such cases; obedience is imperative."[14]

Kant's great respect for the tolerant practices of Frederick II (the Great) is well known. Kant equates the dawning of "the age of enlightenment" with "the century of Frederick." In this essay, written two years before Frederick's death, Kant even makes an allusion to and twice quotes the king: "Only one ruler in the world says: 'Argue as much as you like and about whatever you like, but obey!' " A curious compliment from one who would "walk alone." And though Kant acknowledges that this thesis does lead to a "strange and unexpected pattern in human affairs," he maintains that "a lesser degree of civil freedom gives intellectual freedom more room to expand to its fullest extent." Of course, such an arrangement necessitates that intellectual freedom will need specific criteria for how to distinguish "the guardians," who must be overcome, from the sovereign, who enables intellectual freedom to expand to its fullest extent.

Nevertheless, according to Kant, we have a duty to free ourselves from such immaturity and continue boldly on our way. How then do we throw off the shackles of an outdated immaturity? In a word, it takes courage. It is because of a lack of courage that society now finds itself in this self-incurred immaturity, and even within a reasonably free state, only the forthright exercise of courage will bring about enlightenment. Thus we are brought around to what Kant declares to be the motto of the Enlightenment: *"Sapere aude!"*

---

[14]Ibid., pp. 55-56.

Kant's melodramatic appeal to Horace is problematic, however. Though often translated "Dare to know," or "Have courage to use your own understanding." *Sapere aude* is more accurately rendered "dare to be sensible," or "dare to be wise." (*Audere*—to dare, "audacious"; *sapio, -ere*— "to taste, to have knowledge of." The context for the quotation from Horace speaks to "avoiding extremes," moderation.)[15] My translation of choice is "Be audacious enough to be sensible." These alternative translations lack altogether the heavy-handed exhortation to summon all one's courage so that he or she might achieve intellectual independence. It is difficult to square the Kantian "Have the courage to think for yourself" with the Horatian "Be audacious enough to be sensible." Indeed, to be "sensible" or "wise" has the connotations of participation in a community or the gaining of insight from an intellectual tradition. Insight, wisdom and sensibility are the rewards of maturity and experience; they reflect the learning of a craft, not the courageous exit from the self-imposed immaturity Kant had in mind.

And yet the Horatian motto continues to be the motto of the Enlightenment. What kind of ethic should these mature individuals have? The answer will come from Max Weber (1864-1920), who called the Enlightenment into question even as he confirmed its deepest dogmas. Weberian maturity will demand an ethic of responsibility in a disenchanted world.

Two decades into the twentieth century Weber began his famous essay "Politics as a Vocation" (1918) with the supposedly nonproblematic assumption that all politics must be understood in the context of statecraft. According to Weber, "We wish to understand by politics only the leadership, or the influencing of the leadership, of a *political* association, hence today, of a state."[16] Just as Hobbes rejects any notion of the *summum bonum*, so Weber contrasts the "ethic of ultimate ends" (exemplified in the Sermon on the Mount) with an "ethic of responsibility." Weber's picture of maturity exemplifies this ethic of responsibility, and for Weber, in the modern world, one is responsible to the state. To be a believer in an ethic of ultimate ends is, as Weber correctly notes, an all-or-nothing proposi-

---

[15]Horace, *Epistles* 1, 2, 40. Thanks to Tim Johnson, department of classics, University of Florida, for his help with this passage.

[16]Max Weber, "Politics as a Vocation," in *From Max Weber: Essays in Sociology*, ed. and trans. H. H. Gerth and C. Wright Mills (New York: Oxford University Press), p. 77.

tion poorly suited for the modern age. He writes, "The same holds for this ethic as has been said of causality in science; it is not a cab, which one can have stopped at one's pleasure; it is all or nothing."[17]

Weber recognizes that a state-sponsored ethic of responsibility will inevitably have recourse to violence. Weber notes, "No ethics in the world can dodge the fact that in numerous instances the attainment of 'good' ends is bound to the fact that one must be willing to pay the price of using morally dubious means or at least dangerous ones—and facing the probability of evil ramifications." And again, "The decisive means for politics is violence."[18]

Weber's ethic of responsibility is a "realistic" ethic that seeks to take stock of the world in which individuals find themselves in political communities. Moreover, the world in which individuals find themselves is a "disenchanted world." As Weber notes in "Science as a Vocation," disenchantment is the result of increased intellectualization and rationalization such that "there are no mysterious incalculable forces that come into play, but rather . . . one can master all things by calculation."[19]

Weber's ethic of responsibility should not be confused with his famous examination of the "Protestant ethic." Almost two decades before "Politics as a Vocation," Weber had written *The Protestant Ethic and the Spirit of Capitalism* in an attempt to understand the psychological conditions that allowed capitalism to thrive and flourish. There are, of course, many important connections between that book and the companion essays "Politics as a Vocation" and "Science as a Vocation." Perhaps the most important connecting thread is the notion of vocation or "calling." Confessing that "The Puritan wanted to work in a calling; we are forced to do so," Weber famously describes the modern age as one in which "the idea of duty in one's calling prowls about in our lives like the ghost of dead religious beliefs."[20] The companion essays, with the incumbent ethic of responsibility, seek to make sense of vocation—calling—in a disenchanted world.

The mature man recognizes this reality and responds accordingly. Only

---

[17]Ibid., p. 119.
[18]Ibid., p. 121.
[19]Max Weber, "Science as a Vocation," in *From Max Weber: Essays in Sociology*, p. 139.
[20]Max Weber, *The Protestant Ethic and the Spirit of Capitalism*, trans. Talcott Parsons (New York: Scribner's, 1958), pp. 181-82.

the immature still seek "meaning" in a disenchanted world. Weber asks, "Who—aside from certain big children . . . still believes that the findings of [the natural sciences] could teach us anything about the *meaning* of the world? If there is any such 'meaning,' along what road could one come upon its tracks?"[21] No, Weber's calling is to give up "the grandiose moral fervor of Christian ethics" for an ethic of responsibility and the possibility of making a contribution, however small and transitory, to a world of knowledge and science.

Surely there are others who have contributed substantively to the development of the Liberal notion of human maturity and to the development of the idea that those considerations which matter most to the governance of the modern nation-state should be preeminent for all aspects of our ordered lives together. But the progression from Hobbes to Kant to Weber offers a window on the difficulty of redeeming Liberalism for a Christian understanding of the relationship between the Christian and the state.

As noted at the outset of this chapter, Father Neuhaus believes that I (along with "Hauerwas and Co.") have "a tendency to reify 'liberalism,' turning it into a concrete and coherent doctrine far beyond what many who affirm 'the liberal tradition' recognize as their own position."[22] Surely he would reject my formulation of Liberal maturity as exemplified by an unencumbered self whose highest expression of maturity is the freely willing of one's own will which neither infringes upon the rights of others nor fails to exercise a realistic ethic of responsibility in a newly disenchanted world.

By the phrase *liberal tradition*, Neuhaus intends "something quite modest but nonetheless of great value." He insists that "the firmest foundation of the liberal democratic tradition" is exemplified by the claim "Jesus Christ is Lord. That is the first and final assertion Christians make about all of reality, including politics. Believers now assert by faith what one day will be manifest to the sight of all: every earthly sovereignty is subordinate to the sovereignty of Jesus Christ."[23] Amen. I fully concur

---

[21]Weber, "Science as a Vocation," p. 144.
[22]Neuhaus, "Extraordinary Politics," p. 61.
[23]Neuhaus, "Extraordinary Politics," pp. 62-63, cited in "Christianity and Democracy" *First Things*

with that statement, but I cannot figure out what it has to do with Liberal democracy—besides undercutting democracy's special claims to our loyalties and allegiances. When John Rawls, following the lead of Hobbes, Locke and Kant, argues for the priority of the Right over the Good, he intends to secure a political order in which one's right to affirm "whomever or whatever is Lord" is not endangered by someone else's understanding of what is the Good for society. Rawls believes that such an abstract understanding of the state can be the basis for the most just statecraft that can be arranged.

Is someone who affirms Neuhaus's statement (for instance, someone like me) "mature" and "tolerant" by Enlightenment standards? Absolutely not. Enlightenment maturity assumes a disenchanted worldview; Neuhaus and I have not only consented to the Good over the Right, we have also affirmed the priority of a philosophy (in this case, Christian faith) before democracy. Our confession of faith cannot be the "firmest foundation of the liberal democratic tradition." Neuhaus is attempting to reclaim an abstract notion of the state in the hope of transforming it into what such a state may someday become. Baxter rejects these sorts of formulations. Recall his earlier denial of the church's need for a theory of the state.

> I distrust attempts to provide an account of "the state" in the abstract because such attempts legitimate what is in the name of what ought to be. I especially distrust such accounts in modernity because, as Alasdair MacIntyre has argued, the modern nation-state is a dangerous and unmanageable institution that often masquerades as an embodiment of community and a repository of sacred values. Faced with this situation the church does not need a theory of the state. What the church needs is a description of the true character of the state and a set of practices to resist it. To designate the modern nation-state as an instrument by which to propagate the Christian faith is to imperil the Christian faith.[24]

In Hobbes we get the move from flourishing to prosperity that sets up the absorption of any intermediate commitments (like church or family) by the state. In Kant we get the paradoxical command to use our reason

---

66 (October 1996).

[24]Michael Baxter, "Correspondence," *First Things* 75 (August-September 1997): 6.

and argue as much as we like—only obey. And in Weber we finally grasp the realism that we are called to an ethic of responsibility that must embrace violence. The modern nation-state maintains a monopoly on violence. If we are to reject this inheritance, we will need a "description of the true character of the state" and a set of practices that enable us to "escape the thrall of the state." Extraordinary politics will require courage. We will have to be audacious enough to be sensible. *Sapere aude.*

## LIBERALISM AND "RIGHTS DISCOURSE"

Can the effects of the Liberal reduction of politics to statecraft be seen in our everyday lives? I believe that this can be demonstrated. As noted above, one of my operating assumptions is that the culture of Enlightenment Liberalism has steadily exported its principles, vocabularies and methodologies from the public sphere of government and statecraft (where it works, more or less, pretty well) into almost every other sphere of our daily lives (where it is far less successful). For instance, most of us, without even thinking, use the language of "rights" to negotiate many of our differences with one another. With our spouses, in our churches, at the workplace, we think and talk about our privileges and obligations through the rubric of rights. "I have the right to do this," or "you can't take away our right to do that." (Perhaps the best treatment of this phenomenon is Mary Ann Glendon's superb *Rights Talk: The Impoverishment of Political Discourse.*)[25] The preeminence of rights discourse in our contemporary society is the most obvious contemporary example of the modern reduction of politics to statecraft.

There is nothing inherently wrong with talking and thinking of the human experience in terms of one's rights, but there is nothing particularly obvious about its universal applicability, either. Rights discourse works best in bad situations. This is as it should be. As Jean Bethke Elshtain has noted, it is only after the 1940s that rights talk gets transformed from referring primarily to immunities to referring ever more often to entitlements.[26] Bad situations are those situations in which indi-

---

[25]Mary Ann Glendon, *Rights Talk: The Impoverishment of Political Discourse* (New York: Free Press, 1991).

[26]Jean Bethke Elshtain, *Democracy on Trial* (New York: Basic Books, 1995), p. 15.

viduals or groups are being treated "unfairly" or "inappropriately." It is a court of last appeal and a court to which we should appeal only when we have really low expectations about the possibility of flourishing.

Rights discourse works well with respect to statecraft and within the rule of law. Most of us want our communities to have the benefit of certain services that the government is well-positioned to provide (good roads, safe cities, public services, certain sorts of assistance to the disadvantaged, etc.), and most of us want to be left alone to live our lives as we see fit—so long as we do not interfere with others who are doing the same. (This is of course a version of John Stuart Mill's "harm principle" previously alluded to. Mill thought of this principle as the fundamental plank of authentic liberty. It is indeed an important principle, but its success requires broad agreement on what constitutes harm. In a consumerist society such as ours, a loss of opportunity, a delay or even an inconvenience can come to be viewed as harm. It is not surprising, therefore, that a culture of convenience and consumption would become an aggressively litigious culture as well.) When others do interfere with or wrongly take advantage of us, we want to be able to stop it. Rights talk allows us to do so, and many of our public relationships and commitments are virtually inconceivable apart from these assumptions and vocabularies.

But rights talk does not work everywhere or all the time. Not only is it inapplicable in certain contexts, sometimes this form of discourse only makes matters worse. The institution of marriage offers just one illustration of how rights discourse exemplifies the reduction of politics to statecraft and how this reduction contributes to a particular transformation of the institution in question.

John Witte Jr. has written a marvelous genealogy of the evolution of the institution of Christian marriage.[27] The transformation from "sacrament to contract" does illustrate the fundamental changes which have occurred in the modern concept of marriage. When a married or an engaged couple begins to mediate their disagreements within the rights language of a contractual property dispute, they begin to see successful resolution of conflict as a matter of "guarding their turf." If the husband is the principal

---

[27]John Witte Jr., *From Sacrament to Contract: Marriage, Religion, and Law in the Western Tradition* (Louisville: Westminster John Knox, 1997).

bread-winner, is he entitled (i.e., does he have the right) to spend his money however he likes? It is perhaps his "right" to do as he likes with his money, but the unique partnership of the marriage is harmed by viewing the situation through this lens. Rights talk in a marriage does become appropriate in physically or emotionally abusive situations. A woman and her children not only have a right not to be abused, they have the right to expect protection against domestic violence. But again, this is a bad situation, and one is correct to have low expectations about the prospects for flourishing.

Rights talk can harm a marriage through the subtle importation of alien concepts and the easy adaptation of words that were designed for other purposes. It can engender assumptions about what a "successful" marriage should look like. "Fairness" is usually proceduralism in pursuit of justice, and as such is predictably equivocal. (In chapter seven I will address the vexed matter of "justice as fairness.") Perhaps most people enter marriage with unrealistic expectations of some sort. If marriage is understood principally as a contract for personal satisfaction, it is not surprising that many couples believe their "right to happiness" is abrogated when the idealistic marriage does not immediately materialize. Focusing on one's own rights (rather than on meeting the needs of one's partner) has the potential to damage the fragile marriage even further.

Liberalism's relationship to the institution of marriage is complicated and ultimately beyond the scope of the current study, but the prevalence of rights talk in modern American marriages is an example of the steady march of statecraft. Politics is just the ordered life of the *polis*, and within this *polis* there are many institutions. Work is one, and marriage is another. For Christians, however, marriage is never merely another social institution. For Roman Catholics, marriage is one of the seven sacraments—a visible sign of God's invisible grace; in the Orthodox tradition, marriage is counted among one of the "mysteries." Even sacrament-shy Protestants treat this "institution" of marriage with a special reverence and awe.

However, when marriage becomes just another institution which we assume is best treated in the same way that we elect presidents, negotiate contracts and sue for damages, we unwittingly endorse a rival conception of what this shared life in marriage should be. In the end we side with Robert Frost and acknowledge that "good fences make good neighbors." But good fences do not make good marriages, and they do not make for the best kinds of neighbors either. Frost knew that too ("Something there is that doesn't love a wall"), but, ever the realist (and Liberal), he also assumed that one's best hope consists in foreclosing on one's worst risks.

So it is also with marriage. In order to avoid the real and present dangers of physical and emotional abuse (almost always against women and children who are the most vulnerable), to avoid an oppressive "patriarchy" that failed to recognize, value or encourage the gifts and talents of "neglected partners" (an oxymoron?), we have frequently assumed that marriage must cohere with an Enlightenment sense of success. As Hobbes predicted, success comes to be understood as prosperity and security; it is understood individually and economically. We have rightly come to fear a more communal understanding of a successful marriage because we know that too often the communal understanding of marriage (in the context of the family) means success for the man in a career outside of the home and no opportunity for the woman outside of the home. Surely that, as a limiting option, is not satisfactory.

Of course, the converse is equally unsatisfactory. In the attempt to avoid these legitimate dangers, we now see an explosion of consumption-driven two-income households in which the quest for material goods and personal success through financial achievement frequently sacrifices the common good of the family or community. For the family or community to flourish, the needs of the family must come first. Such a commitment might manifest itself in a variety of ways. If there are small children in the home, what is best for them? Do the material benefits secured through a second income outweigh the goods procured through one parent choosing to delay entering the work force in order to devote him- or herself completely to the needs of the children? Is the parent who is working outside of the home aware of the complexity and isolation engendered by working at home with the children? Is this domestic vocation as respected as other callings, and rewarded in and outside of the home? Extraordinary politics begins with these sorts of inquiries and commitments.

Whatever our sacramental proclivities, we must keep in mind that marriage in the Christian church began as a sacrament—a visible manifestation of God's grace. As such, Christians should think of Christian marriage as fundamentally more than a social institution. They should think of it as a gift that reflects God's affirmation of the world and their spouse as the instantiation of God's blessing. From such a perspective we see how an excessive focus on one's rights distorts and transforms the overall context.

This perspective illustrates the tragedy of the church's gradual abnegation of its role as custodian of the institution of marriage. Surely there are many types of marriages that are not "Christian" marriages, and the nation-state has a responsibility to legislate certain matters equitably. Nevertheless, the government's power to license, dissolve and mediate marriage comes from the church, which gave up the task. When we, the church, discovered that we could no longer manage marriage, we asked the larger culture to do so for us. And they did.

It is important to realize that Enlightenment Liberalism is much more than just rights discourse, but rights discourse is one way that Liberal hegemony over our private lives is both perpetuated and concealed. After a while the unquestioned propriety of thinking of human success and security in terms of rights is just, well, obvious. We don't even have to think about these things anymore, and unfortunately, we usually don't.

## CONCLUSION

Christians like Baxter and Hauerwas are often accused of refusing "to engage in the nitty-gritty world of real politics."[28] Baxter responds by asking, "What criteria should we use in this nitty-gritty world of real politics?" Baxter notes that if one fundamentally assumes a harmony between Christianity and American democracy, "one wonders whether there are any criteria which would lead [one] to conclude that the imperium called the United States of America just might be a counter-kingdom to the Kingdom of Christ."[29] Baxter puts it this way.

If "politics" is described in liberal democratic terms—as an arrangement in

---

[28]Michael E. Dyson, " 'God Almighty Has Spoken from Washington, D.C.': American Society and Christian Faith," *DePaul Law Review* 42, no. 1 (1992): 159.

[29]Michael Baxter, " 'Overall, the First Amendment Has Been Very Good for Christianity'—NOT! A Response to Dyson's Rebuke," *DePaul Law Review* 43, no. 2 (1994): 440.

which the conflicting interests of individuals and subsidiary groups are adjudicated by the state—then substantive religious convictions must be translated into "interests," thus divesting them of any inherent political valence. However, if "politics" is redescribed in traditional theological terms—as the art of achieving the common good through participation in the divine life of God—then substantive religious convictions are central to legitimate political authority, and interest "politics" is not truly "politics" at all, but a cacophonous conflict of wills. Understood theologically, politics entails the ordering of human relationships according to their ultimate end: God. The primary political setting in which this ordering occurs is the church. If the true *polis* is constituted by the practices of assembled Christians called "the church," the "pilgrim City of God," then "faith" is intrinsically political. Christianity does not "work with politics," nor "apply to politics" nor have "political implications." Christianity is *always already* political.[30]

It is important to note that Baxter is *not* suggesting that the church ought to take over the job formerly held by the state. Baxter is making an argument on behalf of neither a Catholic confessional state nor a Christian theocracy. Rather, the argument is that Christians have a priori reasons for believing that any ordering of human relationships (what I have been calling the ordered life of the *polis*) which fails to apprehend its true *telos* in and ultimate allegiance to God is inadequate and destined to failure as a fundamental ordering which makes human flourishing possible.

There are several important implications which follow from this presentation. First and foremost, this means that Christians can never concede Hobbes's claim that the state is the "Mortal God to which we owe, under the Immortal God, our peace and defence."[31] Hobbes's move forever makes faith at best a penultimate concern. It can never challenge Leviathan. As Cavanaugh suggests, when one accepts Hobbes's formulation the church is absorbed into the state, and the state commands one's ultimate allegiance in matters temporal, bodily and physical. The spiritual and eternal can be left to the church, so long as the spiritual matters do not challenge the preeminence of the state.[32]

---

[30]Ibid., p. 441.
[31]Hobbes, *Leviathan*, (chap. 17), p. 109.
[32]Cavanaugh, "A Fire Strong Enough to Consume the House," p. 407.

But this presentation also makes allowances for a commitment to the state as a penultimate good. This is the rendering unto Caesar what is rightly Caesar's and rendering unto God that which rightfully belongs to God. It also means that Christians cannot "pledge their allegiance" to anything less than (or "under") God.

A second implication concerns education and the pursuit and transmission of knowledge of the *polis*. It means that any sociology of politics or political science that fails to consider the supernatural character of the defining *telos* will fail to understand the political association under examination.

Baxter is committed to the Catholic Worker tradition. Baxter writes,

> The Catholic Worker is committed to a concrete embodiment of gospel through prayer, the sacraments, feeding and housing the poor and homeless, and witnessing for peace. The ethos of the Catholic Worker may be summed up as a commitment to embodying the lesson in the parable of the last judgment [Mt 25:31-46]. In that parable, the Son of Man is identified as a king and the virtuous enter eternal life by putting into practice the works enumerated by the king: feeding the hungry, clothing the naked, visiting the sick, and caring for prisoners. Thus, performing these practices is what it means to live under the Kingship of Christ.[33]

It is important to note that all of these practices attend to the body, which cannot be separated from the soul and mind. Not only are the practices of feeding and housing the poor practices that attend to the body, but the practices of prayer and the sacraments also attend to the body. Prayer and the sacraments are not often thought of as "bodily practices," but they are in the truest sense. William Cavanaugh's *Torture and Eucharist* offers a compelling account of how the practice of Eucharist enabled the church in Pinochet's Chile to resist the discipline of the state torture for the thoroughly political discipleship of Christ.[34]

Though most of us in North America do not face the trials and the physical torture which our Christian sisters and brothers in Central and South America have faced in recent years, we are in desperate need of practices that will enable us to "escape the thrall of the state." Just such

---

[33]Baxter, "Overall, the First Amendment Has Been Very Good for Christianity," p. 445.
[34]William T. Cavanaugh, *Torture and Eucharist: Theology, Politics, and the Body of Christ* (Oxford: Blackwells, 1998).

practices will constitute the extraordinary politics which struggles to make sense of a changing world and the changing place of the church in that world.

Extraordinary politics is politics which seeks to solve certain problems but recognizes that these solutions will leave many other questions unanswered, some of which may have had compelling satisfactory answers that will no longer do. In chapter seven I turn toward an examination of how the inalienable right to the "pursuit of happiness" can tragically lead to the development of a culture of convenience and consumption that has lost its capacity to withstand a culture of death. In the concluding chapter, I point toward one bodily practice that informs and assists with the cultivation of this extraordinary politics. It is the practice of hospitality, which Liberalism has difficulty making sense of.

# 7

## EXTRAORDINARY POLITICS BEYOND THE CULTURE OF CONVENIENCE

We hold these truths to be self-evident: that all men are created equal, that they are endowed by their Creator with certain inalienable rights, among which are life, liberty, and the pursuit of happiness.

THOMAS JEFFERSON'S NOTION OF THE "inalienable rights of life, liberty, and the pursuit of happiness" ranks as one of the most beloved artifacts of American cultural consciousness. Pope John Paul II's phrase "the culture of death" drew criticism from some of the same quarters for being hyperbolic, overwrought and unjustified. I want to argue that the irony of our contemporary cultural situation is that we Americans contrive the former in a way that leads to the latter. *Liberty* has come to mean unrestricted freedom of choice, primarily the consumer's choice. We frequently equate the inalienable right to *pursue* happiness with a right to *be* happy, and for many Americans that means a right to a convenient life.

However, in our quest for convenience, we are tempted to forget that life is intrinsically messy and inconvenient.

By juxtaposing our culture of death with Jefferson's immortal words, I do not mean to suggest that somehow our culture has betrayed the good intentions of the Founders. Quite to the contrary, if we assume that the "pursuit of happiness" is a "self-evident" right, a generic endowment from a generic Creator, we probably deserve whatever we get. Even if we do not think of self-evidence in a strict way (such that merely to understand a self-evident proposition is to see that it is true), we are still left with the peculiar notion that it is self-evident that our Creator has endowed us with "the right to the pursuit of happiness." What does this mean in a culture of convenience and consumption? Moreover, how does an extraordinary politics that is not reducible to statecraft nevertheless contribute to reflection on the statecraft which is exemplified in our contemporary culture? The church must engage the culture within which we live, and to it we must respond with faithfulness, integrity and, above all, charity.

This chapter begins with a brief examination of the "culture of convenience." While capital punishment and euthanasia illustrate how such a culture produces a culture of death, the quintessential example of this tragic phenomenon is abortion, an exercise of power and autonomy designed to avoid that most inconvenient of human practices, the rearing of children. And yet we are not without hope. We can combat the culture of death with the extraordinary politics of hospitality, born of the culture of life. I want to conclude by suggesting that a culture of life will almost of necessity be *inconvenient* and that a culture of life is radically incompatible with a culture of convenience.

## THE CULTURE OF CONVENIENCE

In calling ours a culture not only of death but also of convenience, I am faced with two burdens: first, to demonstrate that we do in fact inhabit a culture of convenience, and second, to argue that this culture of convenience can be understood as leading toward a culture of death. First, however, some preliminary clarifications are in order. Widespread convenience is a particularly urban (and suburban), First World phenomenon that must be understood at both the individual and the societal levels. At the societal level convenience has to be understood as a constitutive dimension of consumption. As consumption becomes the rubric through which we understand the stability and security of our social world, convenience and the desire for convenience increase substantially. It follows then that at the individual level, convenience is what makes consumption efficient; it means "not being bothered" in our pursuit of the goods of consumption. Convenience makes an easy thing like consumption even easier.

Convenience is not, of course, a bad thing. Described in Aristotelian terms, it is neither vice nor incontinence (moral weakness). It is perhaps best understood as what Aristotle calls *malakia* or "softness." In book 7 of the *Nicomachean Ethics*, Aristotle demonstrates that just as virtue is to be contrasted with vice, and continence with incontinence, so restraint or endurance is to be contrasted with "softness." For Aristotle, *malakia* is associated with *trupheros*—a luxury or self-indulgence—and as such implies an "inability, reluctance, or refusal to undertake necessary pains and burdens."[1] Already in the fourth century before Christ, Aristotle is declaring to a leisured class that an unwillingness to undertake necessary burdens inclines one toward moral weakness. From our perspective, in a culture of consumption, such luxuries dull our capacities for rightly understanding the obstacles to human flourishing.

A culture of convenience, then, is really best understood as a culture of convenient consumption. As such it is a culture in which its inhabitants believe that, in the vast majority of their daily, mundane affairs, an expectation of convenience is the anticipated, necessary condition of happiness. It is important to note that this expectation primarily applies to the mundane matters of life. Most people recognize that the genuinely significant endeavors that shape our lives require extraordinary expenditures of time and effort. And yet even here there is often a confusion over what counts as an acceptable level of difficulty. The "no pain, no gain" mentality which applies to our exercise regimen frequently gets forgotten when we must make difficult decisions about childrearing, caring for aging parents or working through the inevitable difficulties in a marriage.

Because an expectation of convenient consumption in our daily affairs

---

[1]Terrance Irwin, "Notes," in Aristotle, *Nicomachean Ethics*, 2nd ed. (Indianapolis: Hackett, 1999), p. 265.

becomes for many of us a necessary condition of happiness, this expectation quietly gets translated into a "right" not to be abrogated. A recent television commercial asserts that one has the "right to surf the Internet without unnecessary delays." The culture of convenience relies heavily on a technological messianism which is believed to make these expectations become reality. The "universal remote control" is marketed as the device that will allow us to control all of our gadgets without ever leaving the couch. On this construal, sustained inconvenience becomes a sufficient condition for abandoning an inconvenient practice (or activity or relationship) altogether.

In short, in a culture of convenience the inhabitants expect to be able to order the minutiae of their daily lives through the easy exchange of consumable goods and services; they are exercising their options *on their own terms*. A church in my city advertises itself as the "home of the 30 minute worship service." We have no-fault divorce, no-fault auto insurance, and drive-through lanes at our favorite restaurants and stores (including liquor stores), and even a "drive through, drop-off" lane at the children's daycare.

The culture of convenience is thus first of all a culture of trivialization. This is extraordinarily important because the trivialization of matters of significance allows judgments of convenience to be formative. The more significant the matter, the less relevant the judgment of convenience. The greater the number of trivialities, the more important convenience becomes. We see this phenomenon in a wide variety of cultural practices. Take, for instance, the institution of marriage. It is not uncommon for couples embarking on a marriage to speak of "giving marriage a try" and "to see if this is going to work out." Increasingly, couples cohabit before marriage to test the relationship. Many others enter marriage with a skepticism about its long-term vitality—and for good reasons. Most of the marriages they see fail. Even religious institutions make implicit provisions for these sorts of skeptical intuitions. Some Protestant pastors have modified the marriage vow in such a way that "till death do us part" is replaced with "from this day forward." The transformation of the institution of marriage from holy sacrament to tentative, revocable contract is evidence of its progressive trivialization. In such a culture, judgments of convenience and utility achieve new prominence and give rise to predictable comments like "we just grew apart."

What is significant about the appeal to convenience is that it is almost never articulated. In a culture of thoroughgoing consumption, the value of convenience is self-evident. Moreover, there is a pragmatic utility about the appeal to convenience. The most convenient thing is the most useful thing, which in turn is the most practical thing. The vast majority of reflective individuals recognize that the notion "the end justifies the means" is at best deeply problematic and at worst patently false. But if the issue is a trivial one, and the desired objective one of practical utility, surely the end does justify the means—or so it might seem.

It is important to note at the outset that death qua death is not the intended consequence of this cultural arrangement (although sometimes that is perhaps the case). Rather, since we become inclined to think of convenience as a necessary condition of happiness, then our right to the pursuit of happiness entails a "right" to pursue convenience. Our pursuit of happiness is inevitably impeded by the presence of some inconvenience or collection of inconveniences. Since we in the urban First World are frequently successful at eliminating these inconveniences, especially through new technological achievements, we are inclined to seek solutions of this sort more generally. The issue is not one of malice but of eliminating the inconvenience. Death is an unfortunate consequence of the intruding inconvenience. As such, death ceases to be an affront by becoming an option, occasionally the most convenient option—sometimes the final solution.

In other words, because increasingly we are confronted with the notion that "the pursuit of happiness" is just the pursuit of the stability and security provided by consumption—a very particular sort of happiness—convenient consumption becomes all that matters. At best, this happiness will be neat and convenient and populated by people who will not infringe on our rights. On this construal, liberty comes to be equated with a condition of maximal possibility and independence from any obstacles that might impede our freedom to choose freely both the substance and the form of our lives. In short, the life of liberty becomes exemplified by John Stuart Mill's harm principle, wherein we are free to do whatever we choose so long as we do not harm another.

If something like this state of affairs is indeed the case, then the existence of a culture of death becomes a truly tragic and ironic consequence. Mill's harm principle, one might think, should have kept the culture of death at bay, but such is not the case. In this connection there are three preeminent problems with the harm principle. Earlier I noted the implicit equivocation found in what counts as "harm."

Second, the harm principle assumes that the Good can be defined formally and procedurally. John Rawls's priority of the Right over the Good is the best contemporary statement of this sensibility. Unfortunately, as is often noted, every procedure works toward some *telos* that it seeks to manifest, and thus there are no ateleological procedures. If my liberty, my happiness, is the most important good, then whether I am harming another is subject to redescription. An abortion is not killing an unborn child; it is terminating a pregnancy. The third problem with the harm principle is that the "good" which the principle does indeed manifest is (as previously noted) that of an ambiguous utilitarianism. Here, it is not at all difficult to see how a culture of death flourishes in this context, especially since death is visited upon the most vulnerable, marginal and silent members of society. This is not the good of the vocal many.

We find the culture of convenience pushing toward a culture of death in many areas of our common life together. I want to focus briefly on capital punishment and euthanasia before turning more in-depth to abortion to illustrate my thesis that convenient consumption bequeaths to us a culture of death.

## CAPITAL PUNISHMENT

The culture of convenience as a culture of death is evident in the increasingly unproblematic role of capital punishment in our society. I will not here address the larger questions focusing on whether (or when) capital punishment is ever justified, and I will certainly not enter the turbulent waters surrounding its place in Catholic social teaching. The widespread prevalence of capital punishment is, however, an important dimension of what John Paul II called the "culture of death."

Historically, the death penalty has been employed as a justified action of the state when the state cannot accomplish the three goals of "redressing the disorder caused by the offense": rehabilitation, retribution and the protection of society. John Paul II's statement from *Evangelium Vitae* is familiar: execution is only appropriate "in cases of absolute necessity, in other words, when it would not be possible otherwise to defend society. Today, however, as a result of steady improvement in the organization of the penal system, such cases are very rare, if not practically non-existent."[2]

For those of us who live in Texas, as I do, such cases are not rare. Forty percent of all the public executions carried out in the United States since 1995 have occurred in Texas. We have overcome our qualms about executing women. Though Karla Faye Tucker's execution in 1997 brought national and international attention to the question of women on Texas death row, the execution of women has lost its novelty in Texas. On February 24, 2000, we executed Betty Beets with little fanfare or media attention. Though Texas has lost the dubious distinction of executing more people than all the other states combined, and is no longer content merely to execute more people than any other single state, we now schedule double-hitters: on August 9, 2000, we executed two people, Brian Keith Roberson and David Oliver Cruz.

The frequent use of capital punishment in Texas (roughly once every week and a half) is evidence of the culture of death about which the pope speaks in *Evangelium Vitae*. Mere numbers alone, however, do not a culture make. Capital punishment in Texas is evidence of the culture of death because of the enthusiasm with which its proponents greet each new execution. Support for capital punishment in Texas is less controversial than virtually any other perennial life issue.

Do we kill our inmates out of convenience? With capital punishment (as well as with euthanasia and abortion) there seems something untoward about the propriety of the rhetoric of "convenience." All the elements of the life well-lived as a life of convenient consumption are present with the case of exuberant capital punishment. What was once gravely significant has been trivialized and redescribed in such a way that the action is not only understood to be consistent with other legitimate practices but also useful as a means toward a greater pragmatic utility.

---

[2] *Evangelium Vitae*, p. 56.

The question of convenience surfaces in both arguments and practices that take capital punishment for granted. Some of these arguments and practices presuppose a wide-ranging acceptance of convenience. Increasingly we are confronted with the bizarre economic argument that prison overcrowding combined with the expense of life imprisonment necessitates the use (and expansion) of the death penalty. I regularly hear arguments like this: "Some of these criminals have been on death row for years and years. Millions of useful tax dollars are being spent by the state to keep these criminals alive when they have already been sentenced to die. These dollars could be better used in education, which would keep people off of death row to begin with." This we know to be false. In Texas the average cost of prosecuting and executing a capital case is $2.3 million. The average costs for life imprisonment amount to about $400,000.[3]

Executions lose their perceived significance through sheer repetition. They become trivial and mundane matters that merit only a brief mention on the nightly news. Even at the Walls Unit, in Huntsville, Texas, where our executions take place, large demonstrations (either for or against capital punishment) are the exception rather than the rule. A friend of mine who is a Baptist minister in Huntsville says that usually there are only small crowds that show up to lament or laud the execution.

It seems to me that part of the increasingly pervasive acceptance of the death penalty in Texas is correlated to the widespread popularity of another relatively new law in Texas, one that gives Texans the right to carry a concealed handgun and euphemistically called "the right to carry". Why should we worry about the state carefully and methodically executing a condemned prisoner when ordinary citizens might be called upon to do the same thing in a moment of crisis? In both cases, death is the convenient solution.

## EUTHANASIA AND THE END OF LIFE

Death also becomes the solution for those addressing the difficult questions which surround the end of life. As with capital punishment, it may seem that convenience is not the appropriate category for discussing eu-

---

[3]Hugo Adam Bedau, *The Death Penalty in America: Current Controversies* (New York: Oxford University Press, 1997), p. 402.

thanasia. And yet we find many of the same themes of convenient consumption coming into play in questions about euthanasia as well.

The cover story for *Time* magazine the week of September 18, 2000, was "Dying on Our Own Terms: A Kinder, Gentler Death." The same week, Judith and Bill Moyers presented a four-part series on PBS titled "On Our Own Terms." The Moyerses' documentary focused on "stories of people who have managed to die more comfortably." The title "On Our Own Terms" was Judith's choice for the series. Bill had chosen the title "Living with Dying," but focus groups and surveys showed that "audiences shy away from words like death and dying," and so the Moyerses went with Judith's more "hopeful" title.[4] Writing in *Time*, John Cloud comments on the Moyerses' subjects in the documentary: "If they are lucky, . . . [they] have discovered how to cast light over the shadow of death, in spite of a system that conspires against dying as well."[5] For the Moyerses, the documentary works in concert with an "education and outreach program" designed to promote a "national dialogue about death" to raise awareness of the "end stage care issues" discussed in their documentary. The $2.5 million spent on the "education and outreach program" equals the amount spent on the documentary series itself.[6]

Someone may object that the *Time* feature and the Moyerses' documentary were not about "euthanasia." They focused on stories, stories about hospice, stories about individuals who had taken the initiative and found alternative medicines for pain management—in short, stories about (and this is a quotation) a "growing movement to improve the way we die." This is much larger than euthanasia, but it is consumption applied to death.

I want to be clear here. To suggest that a culture of convenience tends toward a culture of death does not mean that more resources and energy should not be devoted to expanding hospice and improving pain management, alternative medicines and physician education. Quite to the contrary, these are profoundly good things that ought to be available to the medical community and families in need on a greater scale. The problem is with the normalization, redescription and consumptive attitude toward death.

---

[4]Barrett Seaman, "A Call to Action," *Time*, September 18, 2000, p. 74.
[5]John Cloud, "A Kinder, Gentler Death," *Time*, September 18, 2000, p. 62.
[6]Seaman, "A Call to Action," p. 74.

This emerging culture is one of normalization, redescription and consumption. What kind of death do you want? The kind of death we want is intimately connected to the kind of life we want. If a certain conception of happiness is not possible at that final stage, if we can no longer partake in the happiness of the convenient consumption of late modernity, we want no part of it. We *want* to go gently into that good night.

Though some of us are tempted (with justification) to be quite critical of physician-assisted suicide, we must recognize that the poor souls who find themselves in this predicament are there because as a society, and far too often as the church, we have failed to offer them an alternative to the happiness of convenient, painless consumption. And now, at the end of their rope, they literally have nothing to live for. The culture of convenience is not a culture of death merely because death is the most convenient option for these poor souls. If there were an alternative, many would take it. The culture of convenience becomes a culture of death through decades of subtle indoctrination that convenient consumption is the necessary condition of happiness, and this happiness is no longer available to them.

No life issue is posed in more starkly utilitarian terms than that of euthanasia. Especially for Christians the end is good, the end is desired, the end will be relief from months, maybe years, of isolation, pain, anguish and extraordinary financial expense with ever diminishing resources. How can this good and glorious end not justify any means that will bring the anguish to a close? This is the utilitarian inference of the culture of death.

The culture of convenience also tends toward a culture of death for those who think about the dilemmas presented to their loved ones who must ultimately care for them in their time of need. In this context no phrase is repeated more often than "I don't want to be a burden to my children." This mindset, born of love, the best of intentions, and a realistic assessment of the financial expense involved, probably arises less explicitly from judgments of convenience than from a failure of imagination which is itself the product of our impoverished culture. "I don't want to be a burden to my children" frequently means "Because I love my children and I want them to be happy, I don't want to bother them. I don't want to be a bother. Because I want them to be happy—I want them to be able to continue to be consumers, to live lives of unconstrained, convenient, consumption." Our culture of consumption has thoroughly indoctrinated us to believe that if we are an impediment to our loved ones' capacity to consume, we impede their happiness. And because we ourselves can imagine so few possibilities that are not predicated upon consumption, we nod, agree and admit that we too don't want to be a burden to our children.

But we do have the resources for imagining alternatives. Burdens need not be bad. Our children are a burden! A glorious, God-sent burden. Children rip us out of our delusions about what kinds of neat, ordered, convenient lives we can create. Children demonstrate the inadequacy of the category of convenience for addressing matters that matter. Our children are not convenient, and we were not convenient to our parents as children. (Some of us remain inconvenient as adults.) The inconvenience of children should be absolutely irrelevant to the manifest joy that comes to us even as we are profoundly unprepared to receive the gift of this extraordinarily vulnerable *imago Dei*. The child in one's arms shows us the image of God. Our children never thank us for most of what we do for them. They do not even say "thank you" until after several thousand dirty diapers have been changed. They do say the most inconvenient things at the most inconvenient moments. And they certainly do impede our capacity to consume. And precisely herein lies the hope.

If we can receive the glorious burden of our children in their moment of vulnerability, helping them become what God has designed them to be, even as they enable us to become what God has desired for us, then we can also receive those who have already received us, not only our elderly parents but also the forgotten, isolated seniors of our communities, each of them as the glorious, troublesome, vulnerable image of God that they are. The gospel of life gives us the resources to exercise hospitality within the midst of a culture of death.

Not surprisingly, this brings me to abortion.

## ABORTION

Abortion represents the quintessential instance of how the culture of convenience produces a culture of death. All the elements described heretofore are present: unexpected dilemmas, the perception of diminished prospects for future happiness, trivialization through redescription, technological messianism, and the preeminence of consumption and choice. What was once gravely significant is often trivialized and redescribed in such a way that the action is understood to be not only consistent with other legitimate practices but also useful as a means toward a greater pragmatic utility. Even those pro-choice advocates who lament the trivialization of abortion and describe it as one of the most serious choices in a woman's life insist that this exercise of one's freedom violates no moral obligations or duties.

I should be clear, however, that I am not making the ludicrous claim that women procure abortions because it is the most convenient thing to do. Procuring an abortion is in no way a simple or convenient procedure. I am suggesting that, in a culture of convenience, resisting abortion is exceedingly difficult because the having and rearing of children conflicts with the culture of convenience at virtually every point.

To describe pregnancy, expected or unexpected, as inconvenient fails in the extreme to do justice to the changed state of affairs. There is virtually no sphere of human existence that is not transformed by the knowledge that one is expecting a child. Physical and emotional health suffer a sea change with the knowledge and experience of pregnancy. Pregnancy is experienced, moreover, in profoundly inequitable ways. The most sympathetic father cannot fathom the change experienced by the mother, and far too often the mother must undergo this transformation alone. Women in the workplace know that pregnancy and childbirth frequently diminish their prospects for advancement and promotion in their chosen careers, an obstacle expectant fathers rarely, if ever, encounter. Even when pregnancy is eagerly anticipated and desired, reflection on transformed familial relations, self-perception and heightened financial obligations can all become sources of profound anxiety for the expectant mother. And if this is the case even in situations where the pregnancy is desired, these experiences are magnified many times over in those instances in which the pregnancy seems to be an awful mistake.

It is understandable, therefore, that "terminating the pregnancy" would come to be viewed as a reasonable response to the cataclysmic changes brought on by an unwanted or unexpected pregnancy. And yet the very language of "terminating the pregnancy" masks the move to redescription and, ultimately, trivialization. As dramatic as each of these changes are, which of them justify the private use of lethal force? Despite the fact that the challenges of rearing children are every bit as dramatic as those experienced in pregnancy (and almost always more so), very few individuals believe that the private use of lethal force against them is justified. Unfortunately, this logic only extends to the born, not the unborn, child.

During the last four decades in which the abortion debate has raged in this country, "pro-life" proponents have often sought to push their "pro-choice" opponents toward acknowledging infanticide. If killing one's born child is murder and thus unequivocally unacceptable, why is killing one's unborn child a morally acceptable exercise of one's "reproductive rights"? At the heart of this issue is the question of redescription and consequent trivialization. I believe this move to redescription is largely produced by the culture of convenient consumption.

The question of contested vocabulary is one of the most recurring features of the abortion debate in this country. It is most obvious in the labels "pro-life" and "pro-choice," which are neither contraries nor contradictories. Is abortion "terminating a fetus" or "murdering your baby"? Is abortion by dilation and extraction really a "partial-birth abortion"? One encounters contested vocabularies at every turn in the abortion debate. Other pressing moral dilemmas are not beset with this terminological dilemma. With both capital punishment and euthanasia, proponents of the various positions agree in large measure about the character of the act proposed; their disagreement focuses on whether the act is morally acceptable or not. Not so with abortion. Why is this the case?

I believe that the move to redescription and trivialization is a consequence of our culture of convenience. Even before the pregnancy, sexuality itself has been redescribed and trivialized. It is not "consummation" but "hooking up." To separate the reproductive and the unitive dimensions of sexual intercourse radically transforms the nature of the act and the relationship within which it occurs. The surprising reality, of course, is that pregnancy is so often a surprise.

People do recognize that having a child transforms every aspect of one's life, and so the child does represent a profound challenge to both our present convenience and our future consumption. This sensibility is manifest in many ways, most obviously in the "child-free movement," which opposes tax breaks for parents and desires child-free restaurants, parks and neighborhoods. Such phrases as "terminating a pregnancy" or "exercising one's reproductive rights" are natural manifestations of a culture in which one's "rights" are preeminent and the presence of unwanted strangers (in or ex utero) are a potential obstacle to our pursuit of happiness. The uncontrollable is unacceptable, and whatever else children do, they disabuse us of the notion that we are in control of our lives. One *must* have the choice to terminate a pregnancy because living with constrained choices is unimaginable or at least un-American.

The culture of convenience as a culture of death with respect to abortion is most clearly seen in the "self-evident" propriety of aborting children with disabilities or birth defects. This practice is frequently not even contested. The rapid rise of reproductive technologies is part and parcel of a culture of convenience. In prenatal tests like amniocentesis, a fetus "fails" the test if some defective feature is discovered. As Kathy Rudy notes, "In America today, the abortion of the defective fetuses detected by these tests is virtually mandatory."[7] Citing William Arney's observation that "'some doctors refuse to do amniocenteses unless the woman is willing to commit herself, *before the test is done*, to an abortion in case a defective fetus is found," Rudy concludes, "These abortions are not freely elected or chosen by anyone, but rather are ultimately part of the system that grants primacy to rationality, health, and normalcy."[8]

On September 28, 2000, the United States Food and Drug Administration approved the abortion pill RU-486 (Mifepristone). This pill (actually a series of pills) contains a steroid that blocks hormones (especially progesterone) which sustain a pregnancy. RU-486 was designed to make the abortion process easier and more convenient—both for the woman and the doctor. Some doctors who refuse to perform surgical abortions may be more willing to prescribe RU-486. (Though, in the

---

[7]Kathy Rudy, *Beyond Pro-Life and Pro-Choice* (Boston: Beacon, 1996), p. 13.
[8]William Arney, *The Power and Profession of Obstetrics* (Chicago: University of Chicago Press, 1982), p. 183, cited in Rudy, *Beyond Pro-Life and Pro-Choice*, p. 13.

event the pills fail to abort the fetus, law may require the physician to be willing to perform a surgical abortion or refer the patient to a doctor who will.) Some women may want to avoid the ordeal of visiting an abortion clinic, especially if the clinic is the subject of sustained protests. (Though two to three doctor visits are required to insure that the pills have been effective.)

At every stage of its development, those who support expanded access and increased availability of abortion have sought to make the argument that abortion is not really a major trauma. This is a private matter. It is not murder. This mass of cells and tissue is not a person. This is an exercise of one's reproductive rights. It is a private decision between a woman and her doctor.

But even here such claims are false. Contrary to the marketing of RU-486 as allegedly making abortion safer, easier and more private, this pill does not make having an abortion "more convenient." Women who take the series of pills required may experience severe abdominal pain and protracted bleeding for three to eighteen days, and even then the abortion may not be successful. But even a delusional presumption of convenience is enough for most.

The convenient compromises of our culture of death extend deep within even Christian and self-consciously pro-life circles. In a recent conversation with a young Christian woman who describes herself as pro-life, she said to me, "You've got to admit, nine months is a pretty long sentence for just one night's mistake." Such trivialization of life and death is deeply discouraging. Neither the disjunction between the "nine-month sentence" for the woman or death for the unborn child, nor the recognition that she had tacitly accepted the death of even a potential human being because of its interruption of one's lifestyle appeared problematic for this well-intentioned young Christian woman.

As John Paul II notes in *Evangelium Vitae*, "The acceptance of abortion in the popular mind, in behavior and even in the law itself, is a telling sign of an extremely dangerous crisis of the moral sense, which is becoming more and more incapable of distinguishing between good and evil." In this regard, the pope encourages people of good will "to have the courage to look the truth in the eye and to *call things by their proper names,* without yielding to convenient compromises or to the temptation to self-deception."[9]

Surely someone might object to this treatment of abortion as an instance of how the culture of convenience manifests a culture of death. One might insist that everyone recognizes that abortion is a tragedy, but that it is necessary to insure that disproportionate social and economic burdens are not placed on women—burdens which would certainly be placed on women if the right to procure an abortion were restricted. In this most difficult of settings, these matters are simply better left to women and their doctors than to the government.

Two important points need to be made in response. First, to construe the abortion debate as a question of "who decides, a woman or the government?" is to miss two significant insights. First, there are intermediary institutions that play a far greater role in the formation of persons and communities than the government. For a Christian the church is preeminent among these. Second, even at the level of government, the fundamental intention of the establishment of law is the securing of the common good. Laws perform this function whether they establish standards for tax-free charitable contributions, monitor traffic control or protect children from mistreatment and abuse. And the establishment of law as the basis for the common good is itself a principal, though not exclusive, contributor to the development of culture. In the last thirty years, our culture of convenient consumption has so fully legalized and normalized the taking of innocent life that we no longer recognize abortion as death. Christians are complicit in this culture of death when our embarrassment over an unwed teenage mother in the youth group is greater than our compassion for this young woman and her child.

Second, we must notice that to the extent that we are speaking of "social and economic burdens" we are speaking of the culture of consumption. This culture of consumption is manifest in situations of need and situations of plenty. In the former, if a young woman or a family does not have adequate resources to meet the needs of her family, it is incumbent on her surrounding community to address this situation. In the latter, this unex-

---

[9]*Evangelium Vitae*, p. 58.

pected "economic burden" should be celebrated as the blessing that it is. The problem, of course, is that in situations of plenty, most of us rarely believe our plenty to be enough. This is how the culture of consumption manifests itself with a vengeance. We cannot solve the problem of "how much is enough" by escaping biology through a retreat to our self-evident right to pursue happiness. In cases of both want and plenty, men must be willing to assist women by helping to shoulder the glorious burden that this child represents. In every case, whether there is a father present or not, the Christian church must respond with an unequivocal commitment to be a redemptive people who welcome children and assist those who rear them.

The response to abortion must be one of hospitality—not merely retreating to arguments about the "right to life," which only underwrite the assumption that the language and concepts of Liberal statecraft are sufficient to address the need of the church. Christians should not principally rely on right-to-life language precisely because it cultivates the notions of independence and autonomy as the most crucial for flourishing personhood. Our practice of hospitality stands against autonomy and independence in recognizing an essential dependence and vulnerability we share with all members of creation.

In chapter eight I argue that, for Christians, hospitality offers more satisfactory ways of ordering our shared lives together than the cardinal Liberal practice of tolerance. Hospitality is certainly not a super-virtue that will solve all our problems. Actually, it is not a virtue at all; it is a practice. It will not replace classical virtues like courage, temperance and liberality (though it must of necessity utilize all of those), nor is it a replacement for the Christian virtues of faith, hope and love. As a practice, it seeks to exemplify each of these. It is, however, an extraordinary practice well-suited for an extraordinary politics.

.

# 8

# HOSPITALITY AND THE
# CULTURE OF LIFE

IN THE EARLIER CHAPTERS I ARGUED THAT if politics is to be more than statecraft, then it must be demonstrable in a set of practices which grow out of the Christian community of faith and enable that community to escape the "thrall of the state." In this concluding chapter I argue that hospitality is one example of an extraordinary practice that can make extraordinary politics possible. In the Christian and Jewish traditions few practices have been as formative as hospitality. The Hebrew Scriptures and the Christian Old and New Testaments each require an exercise of hospitality to the stranger. The Catholic Worker tradition has made hospitality the hallmark of its work with the poor, and "Southern hospitality" has become a sustaining practice of Southern Protestantism, which demands almost ritual observance. Hospitality, however, has rarely been thought of as a political practice—but it is.

Hospitality is "political" because it informs and sustains the ordered life of the *polis,* and yet hospitality is not reducible to statecraft. Practices are those complex forms of human activity that exemplify and instantiate the virtues. Virtues are those dispositions of character which enable us to pursue the good for human beings. We should think of the practice of hospitality as an alternative to the traditional foundational practice of Enlightenment Liberalism, tolerance. Hospitality is a political practice that can perform important functions not only *after* tolerance has been tried but also *instead* of tolerance in the meantime.

It is not my objective to denigrate the practice and virtue of tolerance in itself. It should be obvious to all that tolerance is a cardinal practice of a successful democratic statecraft. In order to sustain participatory democracy, to avoid violent confrontation, and to overcome xenophobic prejudice and hatred, real tolerance is an unquestionable necessity. Tolerance is the virtue that is professed but not practiced when it is needed the most.

It is my assumption that we should continue to educate for tolerance, but we must recognize that tolerance will not sustain our communities or our conversations in moments of intellectual, moral or religious crisis. Tolerance cannot make contemplation possible, and contemplation (careful reflection with friends who share a common vision of the best possible life) is an indispensable condition of happiness or true flourishing. Tolerance is ill-suited to address deep political controversy because of its tendency to trivialize the deepest disagreements of our contemporary political landscape. Tolerance cannot be the foundation for an extraordinary politics.

## TOLERANCE IN THE FACE OF REASON'S FAILURE

This argument begins where tolerance usually ends—at the moment when we recognize that our conversation partner holds unfathomable assumptions, is willing to consider unspeakable options or has drawn what we take to be irrational conclusions. To address these questions I turn to John Rawls and his magisterial reworking of the notion of justice as fairness in *Political Liberalism*.[1]

Rawls begins the first lecture of *Political Liberalism* with two questions. The first, concerning what is the most appropriate conception of justice for a society of free and equal citizens, lays the groundwork for the project

---

[1]John Rawls, *Political Liberalism* (New York: Columbia University Press, 1993).

as a whole. Rawls follows this fundamental issue with a second, intimately related question: "what are the grounds of toleration so understood and given the fact of *reasonable* pluralism as the inevitable outcome of free institutions?" Combining both of these questions, Rawls asks the question, "how is it possible for there to exist over time a just and stable society of free and equal citizens, who remain profoundly divided by *reasonable* religious, philosophical, and moral doctrines?"[2] This is the goal of political liberalism, the idea and the book.

It is important to see that Rawls does not intend to denigrate the thick, comprehensive doctrines (like religious beliefs) that stand behind and support our public life. *Political Liberalism* is an attempt, in large measure, to show how a satisfactory account of a conception of justice can be worked out which will neither trivialize nor undermine these comprehensive doctrines. Rawls makes this point abundantly clear.

However, already in those opening questions there is an essential ambiguity that plagues Rawls's project and his notion of toleration from beginning to end: how should we understand what counts as "reasonable"? Over and over again Rawls speaks of "the diversity of reasonable comprehensive doctrines," "reasonable pluralism," "reasonable disagreement." The resulting ambiguity does not arise through any failure by Rawls to address the subject. After the opening lecture in which he addresses fundamental ideas, he goes straight to the tasks of defining the reasonable and showing how this notion becomes the basis for toleration.

For Rawls, reasonable persons are those persons who "desire for its own sake a social world in which they, as free and equal, can cooperate with others on terms all can accept." Unreasonable persons, in contrast, "are unwilling to honor, or even to propose, except as a necessary public pretense, any general standards for specifying fair terms of cooperation." These general descriptions are given greater specificity in Rawls's two principal characteristics for the "reasonable," namely, a "willingness to propose fair terms of cooperation and to abide by them provided others do" and a willingness to recognize and accept the consequences of the burdens of judgment.[3]

---

[2]Ibid., p. 5 (emphasis mine).
[3]Ibid., p. 50.

It is important for Rawls that this definition be "deliberately loose" and encompass some doctrines which "we could not seriously entertain."[4] Nevertheless, Rawls is quite clear on this matter: "the scope of what reasonable persons think can be justified to others" leads "to a form of toleration and supports the idea of public reason."[5] Correlatively, Rawls affirms that "it is unreasonable for us to use political power, should we possess it, or share it with others, to repress comprehensive views that are not unreasonable."[6]

The issue is not whether Rawls has produced a satisfactory definition of what is reasonable. Rawls's definition is a good place to start. The issue before us is the security and stability "reasonable" beliefs receive under a regime of toleration. Put another way, what security or stability do unreasonable beliefs receive under a regime of toleration? For Rawls our capacity—indeed, our obligation—for toleration is intimately connected with our recognition that other beliefs are not unreasonable. Again, "It is unreasonable for us to use political power, should we possess it, or share it with others, to repress comprehensive views that are not unreasonable." Note, Rawls does not address whether it would be *reasonable* to repress comprehensive views that *are* unreasonable.

I do not want to get sidetracked into a discussion of rationality. Moreover, I do not want to defend unreasonableness in and of itself. However, I certainly do not want to base my security that I will be tolerated on the hope that my belief will always be recognized as rational by those who do not share it. Rather, we need not solve the material problem of what counts as reasonable—the formal presentation of the problematic will do just fine: once you have discovered that your conversation partner is unreasonable or irrational (however you define the terms), *what do you do then?*

Tolerance, as the essential and foundational Liberal practice, it seems to me, is inadequate to meet this challenge. Tolerance cannot tell us what to do in this situation. Tolerance may tell us what we cannot do, but it has painfully few resources for engaging the other, especially an other who has been labeled irrational, unreasonable, insane, crazy or ridiculous.

[4]Ibid., p. 59.
[5]Ibid.
[6]Ibid., p. 60.

Hospitality, on the other hand, is the sort of extraordinary practice that can tell us *what to do then*.

## THE INADEQUACY OF TOLERANCE

The difficulties surrounding tolerance are well-known. I want to outline briefly some of these criticisms before turning to the case for and against hospitality. I will in no sense make a case against tolerance but rather point out its difficulties and ambiguities. In recent years there has been a virtual cottage industry devoted to the defense and repudiation of the notion of tolerance—much of this flows out of the so-called Liberalism-Communitarianism debate.

The first difficulty with tolerance is that it is notoriously abstract and ambiguous and, as such, invites equivocation. What does it mean merely "to tolerate" those with whom I differ? Is it just a matter of leaving them alone in the hope that they will go and do likewise to me? Whether or not such a commitment will ultimately work depends on what I want to achieve (either for me individually or for the two of us together) and on what is required for our ordered life together—the fundamental question of politics. If the occasion for our confrontation is a moment of intellectual, moral or religious crisis, then "being indifferent" may not be an option.

The ambiguity of tolerance makes it difficult for us to distinguish among tolerance as *social indifference*, tolerance as *personal restraint*, tolerance as *personal transformation* and tolerance as a *community transformation*. When confronted with an irrational and unreasonable conversation partner or neighbor, indifference and restraint are certainly options, and sometimes the first, best options. But indifference and restraint, by definition, do not make community transformation possible.

Restraint with the other is a good first step, but tolerance involves more. Being tolerant also includes, presumably, not having certain unfavorable dispositions in the first place. This is the tolerance of personal transformation. John Horton notes,

> The tolerant person is not a narrow-minded bigot who shows restraint; he
> or she is not someone with a vast array of prejudices about others' conduct
> but who nonetheless heroically restrains him or herself from acting restric-

tively toward them. The restraint involved in toleration is not exclusively of
action but also of judgment.

According to Horton, "The tolerant person is not too judgmental toward others. In becoming less judgmental, a person becomes more
tolerant."[7] This is the tolerance of personal transformation.

True as this is, this notion of tolerance also points to another fundamental ambiguity. As Michael Sandel has noted, a commitment to a nonjudgmental tolerance which brackets problematic theological, metaphysical or other substantive accounts of moral value is parasitic on the
assumption that these very theological, metaphysical or other substantive
accounts of moral value are false. One can only be nonjudgmental about
(or tolerate) the behavior in question if it is clear that it is *not* morally
wrong. Sandel cites the dispute over slavery in the Lincoln-Douglas de-
bates as a case in point. Sandel writes,

> Douglas claimed that, for political purposes at least, he was agnostic on the
> question of slavery; he did not care whether slavery was voted "up or down."
> Lincoln replied that it was reasonable to bracket the question of the moral-
> ity of slavery [that is, to exercise "non-judgmental tolerance"] only on the
> assumption that it was not the moral evil he regarded it to be.[8]

Horton himself makes this point explicitly: "Toleration must observe limits, that is, that there are some things that should not be tolerated and
hence it is no virtue to tolerate them."[9]

A second difficulty with tolerance as personal transformation is its tendency to foster certain sorts of self-satisfaction. My gallant exercise of
tolerance can become self-congratulatory evidence for my own enlightened state. At the same time, my enlightened tolerance easily cultivates an
inaccurate and harmful view of the other as "irrational" or "unbalanced."
In this setting we tend to think of ourselves (and those who think as we
do) as "enlightened" and others as "unenlightened." And none of us, of
course, really take unbalanced and unenlightened people seriously. This is

---

[7]John Horton, "Toleration as a Virtue," in *Toleration: An Elusive Virtue*, ed. David Heyd (Princeton,
N.J.: Princeton University Press, 1996), p. 38.
[8]Michael Sandel, "Judgmental Toleration," in *Natural Law, Liberalism, and Morality: Contemporary
Essays*, ed. Robert P. George (Oxford: Clarendon, 1996), p. 111.
[9]Horton, "Toleration as a Virtue," p. 33.

the problem alluded to in the opening section.

There are several subdifficulties here. I'll mention three. First is the obvious point that just such a posture of openness and toleration closes us off from both serious self-critical reflection and serious engagement with those with whom we disagree. This is what Stanley Fish calls "boutique multiculturalism."[10] The second subdifficulty, of course, is that sometimes the charge of irrationality really is true. Intolerance does refuse to "play by the rules"—the intolerant "won't be nice." As Bernard Williams has noted, "We need to tolerate other people and their ways of life only in situations that make it very difficult to do so. Toleration, we may say, is required only for the intolerable. That is its basic problem."[11] Following Lincoln's point about slavery, there are certain views that must *not* be tolerated because they are pernicious. The third and more comprehensive subdifficulty is that the virtue of tolerance is incapable of cultivating within us a proce-dural capacity for telling the first sort of subdifficulty (the failure to rec-ognize when we ourselves might be in the wrong) from the second sort of subdifficulty (the failure to recognize when the other is in the wrong). This third subdifficulty is a major problem because the solution to this dilemma cannot be a *material* solution (in which one evaluates the claim or belief in question and decides whether it warrants tolerance); the solu-tion must be a *formal* or *procedural* solution. Tolerance is supposed to guide action *in the absence* of knowledge about the rightness or wrongness of the belief itself. The problem, of course, is how—on the basis of tolerance—can one tell the difference?

And this, of course, leads to the final and most substantial problem with tolerance, the potentially self-contradicting impulse the exercise of tolerance requires. This is the so-called paradox of toleration. Tolerance seems to require intolerance in order to work effectively. To be tolerant, we must all be intolerant of intolerance. However, if we are truly to be toler-ant, we must also tolerate intolerance, thereby undermining our motivat-ing intention toward tolerance. Whether this problem is a genuine one or

---

[10]Stanley Fish, "Boutique Multiculturalism, or, Why Liberals are Incapable of Thinking About Hate Speech," *Critical Inquiry* 23 (Winter 1997).

[11]Bernard Williams, "Toleration: An Impossible Virtue?" in *UI*, ed. David Heyd (Princeton, N.J.: Princeton University Press, 1996), p. 18.

merely verbal horseplay is a subject of no small amount of debate. We need not (and cannot) settle this problem here.

More to the point for our purposes, Williams has noted that "if one group simply hates another, as with a clan vendetta or cases of sheer racism, it is not really toleration that is needed; the people involved need rather to lose their hatred, their prejudice, or their implacable memories." According to Williams, to ask for tolerance among these people is to ask for "something more complicated."[12] Williams is both right and wrong in this assessment. He is right that something more than tolerance is needed, and he is right that tolerance is indeed complicated. But I think he misunderstands what his hateful exemplars need. What they need is a hospitality that offers the possibility of forgiveness and reconciliation; and this is both more and less complicated than tolerance.

## THE CASE FOR HOSPITALITY

I want to present a brief case for hospitality by making two suggestions. First, hospitality, considered in a general, nonreligious way as a community-forming practice, has a chance of succeeding where tolerance falters. Second, Christians have a particular incentive to exercise hospitality in that we recognize that this practice mirrors divine action.

What is hospitality? Hospitality is a practice that emerges from what Alasdair MacIntyre calls the "virtues of acknowledged dependence."[13] These virtues are the dispositions of character that enable us first to recognize and then to respond to the vulnerability and the dependence of others. The offer of hospitality begins with the attempt to meet the most dire needs (food, clothing, shelter) of those who are in need through an exercise of self-giving sacrifice.

Hospitality is always particular; it is an offer made to the stranger or the one in need. We can never offer generic hospitality; we always offer hospitality *to someone*. This hospitality is also specifically located in a cultural setting. There is a host and a guest. As such, hospitality invites a narrative orientation to the human life as a whole. The other tells us his or

---

[12]Ibid., p. 19.
[13]Alasdair MacIntyre, *Dependent Rational Animals: Why Human Beings Need the Virtues* (Chicago: Open Court, 1999), pp. 119-28.

her story; we tell them ours. And though we do not always agree, hospitality has a transforming effect on both the host and the guest. Through the exercise of the practice of hospitality, I learn how to become both a cheerful giver and a gracious receiver.

Of course, the practice of hospitality does not always yield outcomes which are immediately understood as positive. Practicing hospitality makes one vulnerable, and there will always be those who take advantage of vulnerabilities. The prudent action might seek security and forestall vulnerability. But avoiding vulnerability is not prudence. According to Josef Pieper, this sort of avoidance is a form of covetousness. He writes,

> Covetousness means . . . desperate self-preservation, over-riding concern for confirmation and security. Need we say how utterly contrary such an attitude is to the fundamental bent of prudence; how impossible the informed and receptive silence of the subject before the truth of real things, how impossible just estimate and decision is, without a youthful spirit of brave trust and, as it were, a reckless tossing away of anxious self-preservation, a relinquishment of all egoistic bias toward mere confirmation of the self; how utterly, therefore, the virtue of prudence is dependent upon the constant readiness to ignore the self, the limberness of real humility and objectivity?[14]

This "youthful spirit of brave trust" and the "limberness of real humility" are beautifully demonstrated in hospitality, which is demonstrable in specific acts of service and compassion. When most of us think of hospitality, we think of its colloquial use. Hospitality is the opening of one's doors, the presentation of one's table and the generous sharing of the fruit of one's labor. As such, it does not suffer from some of the ambiguities and abstractions that besiege tolerance. Hospitality is an affirmative rather than a negative practice. It is active rather than passive. There is no hint or connotation of indifference. If we are serving the stranger, then we are not being indifferent to his or her need.

Hospitality undermines one aspect of the false dichotomy of the public-private split in contemporary life. To invite the stranger into one's home is

---

[14]Josef Pieper, *Four Cardinal Virtues*, trans. Richard Winston and Clara Winston (Notre Dame, Ind.: University of Notre Dame Press, 1966), p. 21.

to make that which is private public, and to introduce what is public into the private. Certain aspects of the distinction between public and private life are important, but they can also become the basis for a misunderstanding of the relation of the self to the social world. By cultivating hospitality as one of the habits of communal life, we disabuse ourselves of this potential self-delusion.

Hospitality also denies the allegedly neutral space within which tolerant political discourse longs to move. Since there is no such thing as neutral space to begin with, this means that hospitality is also more honest. By denying the neutral space and establishing a context of reference ("Welcome to our home. Make yourself at home."), hospitality gives content and substance to moral discourse. When moral discourse is abstracted from any intellectual community or tradition of inquiry, it runs the risk of making grand statements and platitudes about the moral life in ways that do not cohere with the content of the claim.

Hospitality also values persons over rights. The focus on persons rather than rights emphasizes responsibilities over entitlements and shared goods over distributed resources. Rights discourse (as a product of Liberal statecraft) somehow seems out of place in the context of a home where the host serves the guest and invites him or her to partake of its bounty.

Hospitality is a practice to which most major world religions are already committed. As noted earlier, the Hebrew Scriptures, the Christian Old and New Testaments, and the Qur'an all require an exercise of hospitality to the stranger. In each of these monotheistic traditions, hospitality to the stranger is a reciprocal response to the hospitality God has exercised toward us. Each tradition also modifies the concept. In the New Testament, for instance, as John Koenig notes, hospitality refers "not to a love of strangers per se but to a delight in the whole host-guest relationship, in the mysterious reversals and gains for all parties which may take place."[15] As such, hospitality can become a catalyst for expanded interfaith conversation, engagement and encouragement.

The attacks of terrorists on September 11, 2001, and the subsequent "war on terror" have made interfaith conversation and inquiry much more diffi-

---

[15]John Koenig, *New Testament Hospitality: Partnership with Strangers and Mission* (Philadelphia: Fortress, 1985), p. 8.

cult. In these settings one often hears that religion must be laid to one side before any progress can be made. This move naturally follows from a notion of statecraft which can only view religion with suspicion. But is this the only alternative?

What if the international community—specifically the international communities of Christians, Muslims and Jews—were to encourage *greater* fidelity to their religious traditions? Rather than attempting to get the antagonists to bracket their religious beliefs, what if they were encouraged to be *better* Christians, *better* Muslims and *better* Jews? Don't all Christians, Muslims and Jews recognize that the God of Abraham, whom they all worship, *requires* them to treat the stranger (and the alien) with compassion and service? Isn't there a better chance for peace—indeed, for shalom and salaam—than by appealing to a weak commitment to "rights," which is inevitably overshadowed by intractable memories? These communities are in desperate need of practices that will enable them to overcome the thrall of the state.

Would such an endeavor succeed? That depends entirely on what one counts as success. Will it bring an end to hostilities in the Middle East or help forge an abiding plan for peace and stability in this sacred, war-torn region? Probably not—that is a task for statecraft (though statecraft has a poor record here). But if success is understood as broadening the community and deepening its capacity for understanding and service, as taking the good news of God's grace into all the world, and as faithfully responding to that grace, then, yes—its chances for success are quite good.

It is here in the context of hatred that I think we find the most compelling case for hospitality. Hospitality is a Christian exercise that mirrors divine action. Recall Bernard Williams's exhortation: "If one group simply hates another . . . it is not really toleration that is needed."[16] Hospitality turns out to be an expression of solidarity. Mother Teresa and Dorothy Day did not merely say, "Come in. Live with us." They said, "May I live with you?" more adequately reflecting the incarnation in which God said, "I will live with you." That is the transformation that grace works in us as we move from our practice of "come live with me" to God's practice of "I

---

[16]Williams, "Toleration: An Impossible Virtue?" p. 19.

will live with you." The divine face of hospitality is solidarity.

Of course, some will fear that we may forfeit our ability to speak with authority on those subjects for which the culture of death has demanded that we be nonjudgmental. Not at all. Our actions will speak infinitely louder than our words. Doesn't our willingness to live with others give us the authority to tell them something they would not otherwise hear, or want to hear? If we are caring for the unwed mother, sharing her sorrows and trials, what kind of authority do we have when we offer to help her raise her child? If we are befriending the homosexual and sharing his sorrows, what kind of authority do we have when we offer to help him live the life of self-sacrifice called for in celibacy? If we do not abandon the dying, what sort of authority do we have when we encourage them not to despair? There is no either-or between hospitality and solidarity. It is the human and the divine made one in Christ that welcomes and goes out.[17]

Consider how the cultivation of hospitality informs and transforms how one might respond to the three dilemmas presented earlier: abortion, homosexuality and the end of life.

As previously noted, I believe that a rich communal practice of hospitality is more effective for addressing the challenge of abortion than arguments about the "right to life" of the child. I am not opposed to "right to life" arguments, and in a certain sense I believe that they accurately identify that there are members of our community (unborn children) who deserve the same protections we as a community provide to children who are outside of the womb. However, rights talk merely juxtaposes the rights of the unborn child against the rights of the mother. As is always the case with rights talk, there must be another level for adjudicating the disputes between conflicting rights; in this case there must be a hierarchy of rights.

"Right to life" arguments are appropriate in courts of law, but in the everyday world of the church and community, our exercise of hospitality to the unexpected child trumps our hierarchies of rights. *The news that a child will be born is always cause for celebration.* Despite the difficult situations so many children are born into, they are always to be welcomed and

---

[17]I am indebted to John O'Callaghan for this formulation.

celebrated. As Dorothy Day so eloquently put it, "We are people who welcome children." Since there are no greater strangers who come into our lives and change us forever than our children, it is appropriate to understand welcoming children as basic acts of hospitality. This is the case whether it is our own child or that of another, a long-awaited child or the surprise no one expected, the child of the unwed teenage couple or yet another child conceived because of a promiscuous lifestyle.

John O'Callaghan, the Notre Dame philosopher and director of the Jacques Maritain Center, describes children as "the life-preservers God sends to save us that say 'I have faith in you.'"[18] In an unintended pregnancy the child is not the problem. The child is the one good thing in what may be a very difficult situation. The child is the source of hope, and this hope is the hope of redemption. It is often not the redemption we expect or even desire, and yet God's redemption has always come in unexpected and surprising ways, and so very often in the form of unexpected, frequently unwanted, children. Isaac, Jacob and preeminently Jesus Christ himself were unanticipated children sent as God's means for humanizing us, for teaching us what it means to be human, to be created *imago Dei*.

Our responsibility, however, does not end with the child. We also exercise hospitality to the pregnant woman—married or unmarried—and hospitality to the father, responsible or irresponsible. Hospitality to the woman who had the abortion, whether it has brought her relief or remorse. Hospitality to the father who paid for the surgery in the hope that it would all go away. Hospitality to the health-care worker who performed the abortion. And hospitality to the friend who counseled, convinced, drove and assisted the one in need.

Hospitality is the proper practice for addressing homosexuality. One of the difficult aspects of our contemporary political and cultural scene is that conversation about homosexuality and the church is consumed by activism (which is primarily directed toward rights talk). Such need not be the case. I believe that the posture of "welcoming but not affirming" offers an opportunity for genuine Christian conversation and discipleship about our sexual lives. Some homosexual Christians reject this pos-

---

[18]Personal correspondence with John O'Callaghan dated March 25, 2004.

ture on the grounds that where there is no affirmation, there is no genuine welcome. If that response is required, it will be difficult for many orthodox and evangelical churches to exercise hospitality here. But there is more to be said.

I find it shocking how many Christians I encounter who show disgust and contempt for homosexuals. Pointing to scriptural teachings that reject homosexual unions and activities as sinful, some Christians feel justified in their holy hatred. Hospitality is the needed response, which must be directed toward both homosexuals and the Christian brother or sister whose contempt has become commonplace. Hospitality has no *tolerance* for contempt. There is no place for self-satisfied hatred that condemns the homosexual. The exercise of hospitality to the homosexual no more requires one to compromise one's beliefs than exercising hospitality to the heterosexually promiscuous, the gossips or the self-righteous. Hospitality is not incompatible with church discipline—indeed, it may be a manifest sign of grace. If a church member persists in promiscuity or if another is unwilling to lay down hatred, then either one may need to be removed from communion for a time, in the hope that he or she may be welcomed back in faithfulness.

Because hospitality is always specifically located in a cultural setting (for instance, one's home) it means that the host serves the guest, but it does not mean that the host condones or even allows all kinds of offensive actions. Here one sees clearly the difference between hospitality and tolerance. Those who promote tolerance might suggest that an attitude of nonjudgmental avoidance is superior to the engaged service of hospitality which does put restrictions on what one will or will not be allowed at a particular time or place. Not allowing certain behavior may seem inhospitable, but such is not the case. Hospitality teaches us that even service with restriction is superior to tolerated indifference. It teaches the guest to respect the wishes of the one who serves, and it teaches the host how to become an agent of reconciliation in that service.

Hospitality is also the proper practice for addressing those difficult issues that concern the end of life. We exercise hospitality to the one who suffers from illness, to the one for whom life has become a drudgery and to the elderly parent who makes unreasonable demands. Hospitality means care, compassion and abiding respect for those who have lost their ability to control their bodily functions; hospitality means cheerful service without expectation of return.

Hospitality must be extended to those who have not been hospitable. To the criminal who has taken life, to the official who has decided who "deserves" to die, and to the lawyers, judges, jurors and jailers who carry out the wishes of our culture of death.

None of these instances require the abrogation of justice. In none of these instances does hospitality require the compromise of one's belief or the forfeiture of one's commitments. All of these occasions become opportunities for reconsidering how we might instantiate a culture of life in the midst of this present culture of death. All of these occasions become opportunities for welcoming the stranger or the one in need.

## OBJECTIONS TO HOSPITALITY

Hospitality also poses certain internal and external difficulties. There are at least two kinds of objections to hospitality: the reasons why I'm afraid to practice hospitality, and the reasons why I'm afraid for you to do so.

Hospitality is problematic for the host. It requires a lot of work. It is potentially messy, dirty, expensive and thankless. Flannery O'Connor, writing to her friends the Fitzgeralds, speaks of some immigrants who were due to arrive at her family farm and were to live and work there while they settle in. O'Connor writes, "My mama's refugees haven't come yet; she don't know why. She is very anxious to get them here and have the difficulties begin."[19] Little more need be said on this first point. Hospitality is inconvenient. Of course, children, friendship, marriage, work—life itself—these are all thoroughly inconvenient as well.

Hospitality also poses problems for the guest. Like tolerance it may be easily abrogated. Even when practiced, hospitality can become offensive. It can be condescending. Certain forms of hospitality may do more to undermine the cultivation of authentic community than to undergird it. (The aforementioned "Southern hospitality" has been known to function in just this way.) I would object to any action (masquerading as hospitality)

---

[19]Flannery O'Connor, *The Habit of Being*, ed. Sally Fitzgerald (New York: Noonday Press, 1979), p. 31.

that demeans or belittles the guest. Condescension is not hospitable.

As noted earlier, hospitality is also dangerous. To be hospitable is to make oneself vulnerable. That vulnerability can be taken advantage of. However, that vulnerability is also the basis for genuine community.

Perhaps the strongest argument against hospitality is a variation on the theme of the danger of hospitality already cited. This is Gillian Rose's fundamental criticism of Emmanuel Levinas. Rose notes, "I cannot bow the knee to I know not what." In a century filled with Auschwitz, the Gulag, Cambodia, Rwanda, Bosnia and Iraq, this is certainly an apt warning. And yet we must hear Rose's critique with all the clarity of its intention. Her critique is against a certain passivity for the other; it is not against an engaged hospitality. Indeed, Rose returns to make just this point. She sees the widespread appeal of Levinas's work as explaining a certain modern "hope of evading the risks of political community." Hospitality, whatever it is, is no evasion of the risks of political community. She writes, "Without the soul and without the city, we cannot help anyone."[20]

There are certainly difficulties with hospitality. Hospitality quite literally *invites* difficulties. Still there is justification for seeking to cultivate this practice and implement it in our public lives—lives which have been made public through gracious sharing.

Tolerance is the practice which says: "We are willing to put up with you. We don't like you, or your ideas, or your behavior, but we are willing to stomach your sorry condition and behavior in the name of your civic liberty to do and be these things." Hospitality, by contrast, is the specifically Christian practice which says: "We want to put you up. We welcome you to enter our houses on the condition that you let us enter your lives, engaging you about the matters in which we are morally and religiously disagreed, confessing our own limits and sins as we help you confess yours."

## EXTRAORDINARY POLITICS AND A CULTURE OF LIFE

Hospitality is an extraordinary practice that can inform extraordinary politics. The particularly Christian form of hospitality is a sign of our commitment to a culture of life. Hospitality is the means by which we at-

---

[20]Gillian Rose, *Mourning Becomes the Law: Philosophy and Representation* (Cambridge: Cambridge University Press, 1996), p. 38.

tend to the vulnerable ones at the edges, those for whom life has just arrived and those for whom life is slipping away. It is the means by which we treat others, not in the way they "deserve" to be treated but in the way God has treated us.

Most of us are implicated in the current culture of convenience. I know that I am. We can, however, begin to reject certain portions of this inheritance, in the attempt to create a culture of life. If we are going to accomplish this task, we have to realize that our lives and liberties must entail a different sort of pursuit of happiness. In short, we'll have to pursue a different happiness. And because we are pursuing a different conception of happiness, then we should expect that the means to achieve that end will also be radically transformed.

Aristotle speaks of happiness as *eudaimonia*, the flourishing of what a thing was designed to be. This is what I take John Paul II to mean by a "culture of life." We should expect that a culture of life, as John Paul II describes it in *Evangelium Vitae*, will be inconvenient. It will be marked by the practice of those virtues that make possible the life well-lived.

It should also be clear that a project of this sort will require communities that recognize certain goods, and work to achieve, exemplify and manifest these goods. The modern nation-state is not such a community. On some occasions we hear contemporary conservative politicians speaking of the fundamental issue of politics being that of "tempering our liberty with virtue."[21] The assumption here is that we know what liberty is, and we just want it informed by virtue. But we must speak neither of generic liberty nor of generic virtue. Virtues are those particular dispositions of character that enable us to achieve the internal and external goods of particular practices. While courage will always be the mean between cowardice and foolhardiness, it will be different for the Athenian and the Spartan. As Thomas Aquinas noted, courage for the Christian will consist in endurance, patience and vulnerability rather than in the proud arrogance and aggression of the warrior.

Most Christians have assumed that liberty, freedom, was a matter of the right sort of statecraft. When we are critical of our contemporary

---

[21]Gary Bauer, "Fuzzy Morality," *New York Times*, October 8, 2000.

statecraft, namely Liberal democracy, we are frequently asked, "What's your alternative?" I do not have an alternative theory of statecraft to offer. But I do have an alternative. The alternative is that we refuse to tell lies about what sort of society we live in and what sort of people we have become. We are a materialistic, self-serving and self-deluding people to the core. The pursuit of the happiness of convenience makes perfect sense of our lives. But we are not without alternatives. In this culture of death, we have the opportunity to manifest the culture of life—to children, the dying and those condemned to die, among others.

As Dietrich Bonhoeffer reminded us, there is no cheap grace.[22] To extend the hospitality of the culture of life is hard, tiring, inconvenient work. It leaves no place for sentimentality. We are called to the work by which we learn what it means to flourish—what it means to be and become the kind of people that God has created us to be.

In the midst of our culture of death, what is demanded of Christians today is an extraordinary politics which will enable us to escape "the thrall of the state." Such a politics does not celebrate independence but rather dependence—dependence on God and God's people, the body of Christ. Such a declaration of dependence must be a bold, honest acknowledgment that the holy happiness we pursue is neither self-evident nor convenient. Rather, it is the happiness that God has created us to be, a happiness made possible and announced to us as good news—the gospel of life.

---

[22]Dietrich Bonhoeffer, *The Cost of Discipleship*, trans. R. H. Fuller (New York: Collier, 1959), pp. 45-60.

# Index